TEACHING WITH
poverty
IN MIND

TEACHING WITH

poverty

IN MIND

What Being Poor
Does to Kids' Brains and
What Schools Can Do About It

ERIC JENSEN

Alexandria, Virginia

1703 N. Beauregard St. • Alexandria, VA 22311 1714 USA
Phone: 800-933-2723 or 703-578-9600 • Fax: 703-575-5400
Web site: www.ascd.org • E-mail: member@ascd.org
Author guidelines: www.ascd.org/write

Gene R. Carter, *Executive Director;* Nancy Modrak, *Publisher;* Scott Willis, *Director, Book Acquisitions & Development;* Julie Houtz, *Director, Book Editing & Production;* Miriam Goldstein, *Editor;* Sima Jaafar, *Senior Graphic Designer;* Mike Kalyan, *Production Manager;* Cynthia Stock, *Typesetter;* Sarah Plumb, *Production Specialist*

Printed in the United States of America. Cover art © 2009 by ASCD. ASCD publications present a variety of viewpoints. The views expressed or implied in this book should not be interpreted as official positions of the Association.

All Web links in this book are correct as of the publication date below but may have become inactive or otherwise modified since that time. If you notice a deactivated or changed link, please e-mail books@ascd.org with the words "Link Update" in the subject line. In your message, please specify the Web link, the book title, and the page number on which the link appears.

PAPERBACK ISBN: 978-1-4166-0884-4   ASCD product #109074   n11/09
Also available as an e-book (see Books in Print for the ISBNs).

Quantity discounts for the paperback edition only: 10–49 copies, 10%; 50+ copies, 15%; for 1,000 or more copies, call 800-933-2723, ext. 5634, or 703-575-5634. For desk copies: member@ascd.org.

Library of Congress Cataloging-in-Publication Data

Jensen, Eric, 1950–
  Teaching with poverty in mind : what being poor does to kids' brains and what schools can do about it / Eric Jensen.
      p.   cm.
  Includes bibliographical references and index.
  ISBN 978-1-4166-0884-4 (pbk. : alk. paper)
  1. Poor children—Education—United States. 2. Poverty—United States.
3. Educational equalization—United States. I. Title.
  LC4091.J46 2009
  371.826'9420973—dc22
                                                                2009028621

20 19 18 17 16 15 14 13 12 11 10   2 3 4   5 6 7 8 9 10 11 12

Teaching with Poverty in Mind

Introduction

I grew up in a typical middle-class home. Although the world of the wealthy was appealing to me, what interested me more was the world of the poor. "Why?" was the primary question I grappled with over the years. I was simply unable to fathom why the poor could (or would) not lift themselves out of poverty. I believed that if "those people" simply tried harder or had "better values," they would be able to succeed.

Today, I realize that this attitude was terribly small-minded and prejudiced. But I had to discover that on my own. Extensive education and travel opened my eyes and transformed my soul. Today, I know much more about what goes on in economically disadvantaged families.

This evolution in my thinking is not what drove me to write this book. Instead, I was inspired by this stunningly simple question: "If life experiences can change poor kids for the worse, can't life experiences also change them for the better?" Seeing and hearing how kids from desperate home circumstances succeeded in schools around the world intrigued me. More than two decades ago, I cofounded an academic enrichment program called SuperCamp that has changed tens of thousands of lives worldwide, so I know change can and does happen. My own success and that of others inspired me to find out *how* it happens—and how it can be replicated.

This book focuses on the relationship between academic achievement and low socioeconomic status (SES). In it, I make the following three claims:

- Chronic exposure to poverty causes the brain to physically change in a detrimental manner.
- Because the brain is designed to adapt from experience, it can also change for the better. In other words, poor children can experience emotional, social, and academic success.
- Although many factors affect academic success, certain key ones are especially effective in turning around students raised in poverty.

In this book, I discuss these key factors, highlight real schools that possess these factors, and provide a template for success with specific research-based action steps. If a strategy makes the difference between learning and not learning, it's crucial. Here, I share such knockout factors as well as the research behind them.

About that research. Researchers often claim, "This is what works." But for whom? Low-income, middle-income, or upper-income kids? Was the study conducted over a few weeks, or did the researchers record longitudinal data for 10 years after graduation? What does the phrase *highly effective teachers* mean? Did these teachers' students earn high scores on standardized tests? Or did they enjoy overall success in life? Is the recommended strategy sufficient in itself for success? Is it *necessary* for success? If so, is it necessary for *all* students? Too many sources fail to elucidate these factors and boil down the research to clear strategies that busy educators can apply directly in their practice. That's a gap that this book aims to fill. Here, I focus on the few things that matter most; take any one of these factors out, and you're likely to fail.

Why is there such a stark disparity in academic achievement between low-SES and well-off students? Theories explaining why economically disadvantaged students underperform in school abound: their parents do not have high IQs, their home environment is substandard, their parents are missing or have moved, or they just don't care. Yet these assumptions just perpetuate the problem. A proportion of kids raised in poverty *do* succeed, so we know that a high income level is not a necessary and sufficient condition for academic success. It's true that many poor students have *not* succeeded, but that's due less to parents than to certain school-site variables that may surprise you.

This book offers a three-pronged approach. First, it provides a better understanding of what poverty is and how it affects the students you work with. You'll learn more about the social, cognitive, health-related, and stress-related challenges that economically disadvantaged kids face every day. Second, it demonstrates what actually drives change, both at the macro level (within a school) and at the micro level (inside a student's brain). You'll learn about turnaround schools as well as schools that have a history of high performance among students raised in poverty. The better you understand how to bring about change, the better you can engage the resources necessary to make it happen. Finally, this book addresses you and your school. What can you learn from those who have succeeded? What practices are replicable? Which instructional strategies will help you make miracles happen?

In this book, I aim to provide more than a framework. I give you the theory, the research, and the strategies to ensure success at your school. What I do *not* aim to provide is an exhaustive compendium of every idea on reform, every instructional strategy, and every consultant's opinion on cultural differences. This book assumes you already know that leadership counts, that a healthy environment is crucial, that you should use effective pedagogy, that school safety is number one, and so on. Here you'll learn about what will give you an edge. Think of this book as a spotlight focusing attention on what matters most. I hope that the strategies offered in this book, distilled from my own experience and research, will provide an inspiring and practical guide for improving the lives of your own students.

1

Understanding the Nature of Poverty

Chris Hawkins teaches history in a high-poverty secondary school. He's been teaching for 14 years and believes he's a good teacher. But he gets frustrated in his classes and hits a wall of despair at least once a week. His complaints about his students are common among many who teach economically disadvantaged students: chronic tardiness, lack of motivation, and inappropriate behavior. Mr. Hawkins complains that his students act out, use profanity, and disrespect others. "It's like going to war every day," he says. The recurring thought that goes through his mind is "Retirement is only six years away."

How would you feel if your son or daughter were a student in Mr. Hawkins's class? Only two short generations ago, policymakers, school leaders, and teachers commonly thought of children raised in poverty with sympathy but without an understanding of how profoundly their chances for success were diminished by their situation. Today, we have a broad research base that clearly outlines the ramifications of living in poverty as well as evidence of schools that do succeed with economically disadvantaged students. We can safely say that we have no excuse to let any child fail. Poverty calls for key information and smarter strategies, not resignation and despair.

What Is Poverty?

The word *poverty* provokes strong emotions and many questions. In the United States, the official poverty thresholds are set by the Office of Management and Budget (OMB). Persons with income less than that deemed sufficient to purchase basic needs—food, shelter, clothing, and other essentials—are designated as poor. In reality, the cost of living varies dramatically based on geography; for example, people classified as poor in San Francisco might not feel as poor if they lived in Clay County, Kentucky. I define poverty as *a chronic and debilitating condition that results from multiple adverse synergistic risk factors and affects the mind, body, and soul.* However you define it, poverty is complex; it does not mean the same thing for all people. For the purposes of this book, we can identify six types of poverty: situational, generational, absolute, relative, urban, and rural.

- **Situational poverty** is generally caused by a sudden crisis or loss and is often temporary. Events causing situational poverty include environmental disasters, divorce, or severe health problems.
- **Generational poverty** occurs in families where at least two generations have been born into poverty. Families living in this type of poverty are not equipped with the tools to move out of their situations.
- **Absolute poverty,** which is rare in the United States, involves a scarcity of such necessities as shelter, running water, and food. Families who live in absolute poverty tend to focus on day-to-day survival.
- **Relative poverty** refers to the economic status of a family whose income is insufficient to meet its society's average standard of living.
- **Urban poverty** occurs in metropolitan areas with populations of at least 50,000 people. The urban poor deal with a complex aggregate of chronic and acute stressors (including crowding, violence, and noise) and are dependent on often-inadequate large-city services.
- **Rural poverty** occurs in nonmetropolitan areas with populations below 50,000. In rural areas, there are more single-guardian households, and families often have less access to services, support for disabilities, and quality education opportunities. Programs to encourage transition from welfare to work are problematic in remote rural areas, where job opportunities are few (Whitener, Gibbs, & Kusmin, 2003). The rural poverty rate is growing and has exceeded the urban rate every year since data collection began in the 1960s. The difference between the two poverty rates has averaged about 5 percent for the last 30 years, with urban rates near 10–15 percent and rural rates near 15–20 percent (Jolliffe, 2004).

The Effects of Poverty

Poverty involves a complex array of risk factors that adversely affect the population in a multitude of ways. The four primary risk factors afflicting families living in poverty are

- Emotional and social challenges.
- Acute and chronic stressors.
- Cognitive lags.
- Health and safety issues.

Graber and Brooks-Gunn (1995) estimated that in 1995, 35 percent of poor families experienced six or more risk factors (such as divorce, sickness, or eviction); only 2 percent experienced no risk factors. In contrast, only 5 percent of well-off families experienced six or more risk factors, and 19 percent experienced none.

The aggregate of risk factors makes everyday living a struggle; they are multifaceted and interwoven, building on and playing off one another with a devastatingly synergistic effect (Atzaba-Poria, Pike, & Deater-Deckard, 2004). In other words, one problem created by poverty begets another, which in turn contributes to another, leading to a seemingly endless cascade of deleterious consequences. A head injury, for example, is a potentially dire event for a child living in poverty. With limited access to adequate medical care, the child may experience cognitive or emotional damage, mental illness, or depression, possibly attended with denial or shame that further prevents the child from getting necessary help; impairments in vision or hearing that go untested, undiagnosed, and untreated; or undiagnosed behavior disorders, such as AD/HD or oppositional personality disorder.

It's safe to say that poverty and its attendant risk factors are damaging to the physical, socioemotional, and cognitive well-being of children and their families (Klebanov & Brooks-Gunn, 2006; Sapolsky, 2005). Data from the Infant Health and Development Program show that 40 percent of children living in chronic poverty had deficiencies in at least two areas of functioning (such as language and emotional responsiveness) at age 3 (Bradley et al., 1994). The following two sections examine how inferior provisions both at home and at school place poor children at risk for low academic performance and failure to complete school.

Poverty at Home

Compared with well-off children, poor children are disproportionately exposed to adverse social and physical environments. Low-income neighborhoods are likely to have lower-quality social, municipal, and local services. Because of greater traffic volume, higher crime rates, and less playground safety—to name but a few factors—poor neighborhoods are more hazardous and less likely to contain green space than well-off neighborhoods are. Poor children often breathe contaminated air and drink impure water. Their households are more crowded, noisy, and physically deteriorated, and they contain a greater number of safety hazards (National Commission on Teaching and America's Future [NCTAF], 2004).

Although childhood is generally considered to be a time of joyful, carefree exploration, children living in poverty tend to spend less time finding out about the world around them and more time struggling to survive within it. Poor children have fewer and less-supportive networks than their more affluent counterparts do; live in neighborhoods that are lower in social capital; and, as adolescents, are more likely to rely on peers than on adults for social and emotional support. Low-SES children also have fewer cognitive-enrichment opportunities. They have fewer books at home, visit the library less often, and spend considerably more time watching TV than their middle-income counterparts do (Kumanyika & Grier, 2006).

Often, poor children live in chaotic, unstable households. They are more likely to come from single-guardian homes, and their parents or caregivers tend to be less emotionally responsive (Blair et al., 2008; Evans, Gonnella, Marcynyszyn, Gentile, & Salpekar, 2005). Single parenthood strains resources and correlates directly with poor school attendance, lower grades, and lower chances of attending college (Xi & Lal, 2006). Contrast these children with their peers living in stable two-parent families, who have more access to financial resources and parental time, receive more supervision, participate in more extracurricular activities, and do better in school (Evans, 2004).

Young children are especially vulnerable to the negative effects of change, disruption, and uncertainty. Developing children need reliable caregivers who offer high predictability, or their brains will typically develop adverse adaptive responses. Chronic socioeconomic deprivation can create environments that undermine the development of self and the capacity for self-determination and self-efficacy. Compared with their more affluent peers, low-SES children form more stress-ridden attachments with parents, teachers, and adult caregivers and have difficulty establishing rewarding friendships with children their own age. They are more likely than well-off children to believe that their parents are uninterested in their activities, to receive less positive reinforcement from teachers and less homework help from babysitters, and to experience more turbulent or unhealthy friendships (Evans & English, 2002).

Common issues in low-income families include depression, chemical dependence, and hectic work schedules—all factors that interfere with the healthy attachments that foster children's self-esteem, sense of mastery of their environment, and optimistic attitudes. Instead, poor children often feel isolated and unloved, feelings that kick off a downward spiral of unhappy life events, including poor academic performance, behavioral problems, dropping out of school, and drug abuse. These events tend to rule out college as an option and perpetuate the cycle of poverty. Figure 1.1 shows how

1.1 Adverse Childhood Experiences Model

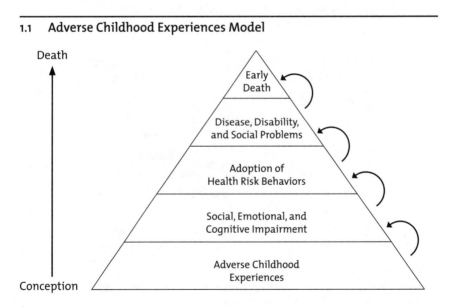

Source: Adapted from "Relationship of Childhood Abuse and Household Dysfunction to Many of the Leading Causes of Death in Adults: The Adverse Childhood Experiences (ACE) Study," by V. J. Felitti, R. F. Anda, D. Nordenberg, D. F. Williamson, A. M. Spitz, V. Edwards, et al., 1998, *American Journal of Preventive Medicine*, 14(4), pp. 245–258.

adverse childhood experiences can set off an avalanche of negative life experiences, including social, emotional, and cognitive impairment; adoption of risky behaviors; disease, disability, and social problems; and, in the worst cases, early death. Figure 1.2 demonstrates the negative correlation between adverse risk factors and academic achievement.

Poverty at School

Studies of risk and resilience in children have shown that family income correlates significantly with children's academic success, especially during the preschool, kindergarten, and primary years (van Ijzendoorn, Vereijken, Bakermans-Kranenburg, & Riksen-Walraven, 2004). Due to issues of transportation, health care, and family care, high tardy rates and absenteeism are common problems among poor students. Unfortunately, absenteeism is the factor most closely correlated with dropout rates. School can help turn children's lives around, but only if the children show up.

1.2   Adverse Economic Risk Factors and Academic Correlations

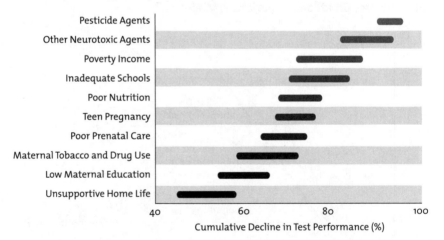

According to this study, each of these factors represents a "risk cost" of 5–15 percent. The factors are correlative, not causal, but taken together they result in a precipitous drop in test performance.

Source: Adapted from "Environmental Toxicants and Developmental Disabilities: A Challenge for Psychologists," by S. M. Koger, T. Schettler, and B. Weiss, 2005, *American Psychologist, 60*(3), pp. 243–255.

Attendance problems often indicate negative parent attitudes toward school. Parents who did poorly in school themselves may have a negative attitude about their children's schools (Freiberg, 1993) and, in an effort to protect them, may even discourage their children from participating (Morrison-Gutman & McLoyd, 2000). These parents are often unwilling to get involved in school functions or activities, to contact the school about academic concerns, or to attend parent-teacher conferences (Morrison-Gutman & McLoyd, 2000). Poor children are also more likely than well-off children are to attend poorly maintained schools with less-qualified teachers, and their day-care facilities—if available at all—are less adequate (NCTAF, 2004).

In addition, in many cases, low-achieving high school students report a sense of alienation from their schools. Believing that no one cares or that their teachers don't like them or talk down to them, students will often give up on academics (Mouton & Hawkins, 1996). Kids raised in poverty are more likely to lack—and need—a caring, dependable adult in their lives, and often it's teachers to whom children look for that support.

Action Steps

Deepen staff understanding. It's crucial for educators to keep in mind the many factors, some of them invisible, that play a role in students' classroom actions. Many nonminority or middle-class teachers cannot understand why children from poor backgrounds act the way they do at school. Teachers don't need to come from their students' cultures to be able to teach them, but empathy and cultural knowledge are essential. Therefore, an introduction to how students are affected by poverty is highly useful.

Consider summarizing information from this chapter or other sources and sharing it with staff. Hold discussions at staff meetings that inform and inspire. Form study groups to explore the brain-based physiological effects of chronic poverty. Debunk the myths among staff members who grew up in middle-class or upper-middle-class households. For example, some teachers perceive certain behaviors typical of low-SES children as "acting out," when often the behavior is a symptom of the effects of poverty and indicates a condition such as a chronic stress disorder. Such disorders alter students' brains (Ford, Farah, Shera, & Hurt, 2007) and often lead to greater impulsivity and poor short-term memory. In the classroom, this translates into blurting, acting before asking permission, and forgetting what to do next.

Change the school culture from pity to empathy. When staff members work with children raised in poverty, a common observation is "Bless their hearts, they come from such terrible circumstances." The problem with that sentiment is that it leads to lowered expectations. Encourage teachers to feel empathy rather than pity; kids will appreciate your ability to know what it's like to be in their shoes. Establish a school culture of caring, not of giving up. You can help foster such a culture by speaking respectfully, not condescendingly, of and to your student population, and by using positive affirmations, both vocally and through displays and posters.

Embracing a New Mission

Beyond its effects on individual children, poverty affects families, schools, and communities (Bradley & Corwyn, 2002). And the problem promises to get worse. Children of immigrants make up 22 percent of the total child poverty cases in the United States (Rector, 2005), and immigration rates continue to increase. Because of the massive influx of immigrants entering the United States every year, the ensuing competition for low-wage jobs, and the statistical link between low-wage earners and increased childbearing (Schultz, 2005), the number of U.S. children in low-income situations is forecast to rise over the next few decades.

We need to address this rising problem, and soon. The timing and duration of poverty matter. Children who experience poverty during their preschool and early school years experience lower rates of school completion than children and adolescents who experience poverty only in later years. In addition, for those who live below the poverty line for multiple years and receive minimal support or interventions, each year of life "carries over" problems from the prior year. Ultimately, these translate to earlier mortality rates (Felitti et al., 1998).

But there is hope. I present research findings in the next few chapters that suggest that early childhood interventions can be quite potent in reducing poverty's impact. Schools around the world are succeeding with poor students, and yours can, too. We must end the cycle of blame and resignation and embrace a new mission to help all our students fulfill their potential.

2

How Poverty Affects Behavior
and Academic Performance

In Chapter 1, we were introduced to history teacher Chris Hawkins. The family Mr. Hawkins grew up in was far from poor: his father was a colonel in the U.S. Air Force, and his mother was a store manager. He had no clue what growing up in poverty was like, and he was shocked to learn about what typically goes on (and doesn't go on) in the homes of his kids. He has learned that there's far more behind the apathetic or aggressive behaviors, commonly attributed to a lack of politeness or dismissed as "lower-class" issues, than he had assumed. What he's learned about his students has depressed and discouraged him. The mantra that gets him through the year is the thought that retirement is only six years away.

The Risk Factors of Poverty

There is no shortage of theories explaining behavior differences among children. The prevailing theory among psychologists and child development specialists is that behavior stems from a combination of genes and environment. Genes begin the process: behavioral geneticists commonly claim that DNA accounts for 30–50 percent of our behaviors (Saudino, 2005), an estimate that leaves 50–70 percent explained by environment.

This tidy division of influencing factors may be somewhat misleading, however. First, the effects of the nine months a child spends in utero are far from negligible, especially on IQ (Devlin, Daniels, & Roeder, 1997). Factors such as quality of prenatal care, exposure to toxins, and stress have a strong influence on the developing child. In addition, the relatively new field of *epigenetics*—the study of heritable changes in gene function that occur without a change in primary DNA sequence—blurs the line between nature and nurture. Environment affects the receptors on our cells, which send messages to genes, which turn various functional switches on or off. It's like this: like light switches, genes can be turned on or off. When they're switched on, they send signals that can affect the processes or structures in individual cells. For example, lifting weights tells the genes to "turn on" the signal to build muscle tissue. Genes can be either activated or shut off by a host of other environmental factors, such as stress and nutrition. These switches can either strengthen or impair aggression, immune function, learning, and memory (Rutter, Moffitt, & Caspi, 2006).

Recent evidence (Harris, 2006) suggests that the complex web of social relationships students experience—with peers, adults in the school, and family members—exerts a much greater influence on their behavior than researchers had previously assumed. This process starts with students' core relationships with parents or primary caregivers in their lives, which form a personality that is either secure and attached or insecure and unattached. Securely attached children typically behave better in school (Blair et al., 2008). Once students are in school, the dual factors of socialization and social status contribute significantly to behavior. The school socialization process typically pressures students to be like their peers or risk social rejection, whereas the quest for high social status drives students to attempt to differentiate themselves in some areas—sports, personal style, sense of humor, or street skills, for example.

Socioeconomic status forms a huge part of this equation. Children raised in poverty rarely choose to behave differently, but they are faced daily with overwhelming challenges that affluent children never have to confront, and their brains have adapted to suboptimal conditions in ways that undermine good school performance. Let's revisit the most significant risk factors affecting children raised in poverty, which I discussed in Chapter 1 (the word *EACH* is a handy mnemonic):

- Emotional and Social Challenges.
- Acute and Chronic Stressors.
- Cognitive Lags.
- Health and Safety Issues.

Combined, these factors present an extraordinary challenge to academic and social success. This reality does not mean that success in school or life is impossible. On the contrary, a better understanding of these challenges points to actions educators can take to help their less-advantaged students succeed.

Emotional and Social Challenges

Many low-SES children face emotional and social instability. Typically, the weak or anxious attachments formed by infants in poverty become the basis for full-blown insecurity during the early childhood years. Very young children require healthy learning and exploration for optimal brain development. Unfortunately, in impoverished families there tends to be a higher prevalence of such adverse factors as teen motherhood, depression, and inadequate health care, all of which lead to decreased sensitivity toward the infant (van Ijzendoorn et al., 2004) and, later, poor school performance and behavior on the child's part.

Theory and Research

Beginning at birth, the attachment formed between parent and child predicts the quality of future relationships with teachers and peers (Szewczyk-Sokolowski, Bost, & Wainwright, 2005) and plays a leading role in the development of such social functions as curiosity, arousal, emotional regulation, independence, and social competence (Sroufe, 2005). The brains of infants are hardwired for only six emotions: joy, anger, surprise, disgust, sadness, and fear (Ekman, 2003). To grow up emotionally healthy, children under 3 need

- A strong, reliable primary caregiver who provides consistent and unconditional love, guidance, and support.
- Safe, predictable, stable environments.
- Ten to 20 hours each week of harmonious, reciprocal interactions. This process, known as *attunement*, is most crucial during the first 6–24 months of infants' lives and helps them develop a wider range of healthy emotions, including gratitude, forgiveness, and empathy.
- Enrichment through personalized, increasingly complex activities.

Children raised in poverty are much less likely to have these crucial needs met than their more affluent peers are and, as a result, are subject to some grave consequences. Deficits in these areas inhibit the production of new brain cells, alter the path of maturation, and rework the healthy neural circuitry in children's brains, thereby undermining emotional and social development and predisposing them to emotional dysfunction (Gunnar, Frenn, Wewerka, & Van Ryzin, 2009; Miller, Seifer, Stroud, Sheinkopf, & Dickstein, 2006).

The need for human contact and warmth is well established. A study of infants in Irish foundling homes in the early 1900s found that of the 10,272 infants admitted to homes with minimal or absent maternal nurturing over a 25-year period, only 45 survived. Most of the survivors grew into pathologically unstable and socially problem-ridden adults (Joseph, 1999).

In many poor households, parental education is substandard, time is short, and warm emotions are at a premium—all factors that put the attunement process at risk (Feldman & Eidelman, 2009; Kearney, 1997; Segawa, 2008). Caregivers tend to be overworked, overstressed, and authoritarian with children, using the same harsh disciplinary strategies used by their own parents. They often lack warmth and sensitivity (Evans, 2004) and fail to form solid, healthy relationships with their children (Ahnert, Pinquart, & Lamb, 2006).

In addition, low-income caregivers are typically half as likely as higher-income parents are to be able to track down where their children are in the neighborhood (Evans, 2004), and frequently they do not know the names of their children's teachers or friends. One study found that only 36 percent of low-income parents were involved in three or more school activities on a regular basis, compared with 59 percent of parents above the poverty line (U.S. Department of Health and Human Services, 2000).

Low-SES children are often left home to fend for themselves and their younger siblings while their caregivers work long hours; compared with their well-off peers, they spend less time playing outdoors and more time watching television and are less likely to participate in after-school activities (U.S. Census Bureau, 2000). Unfortunately, children won't get the model for how to develop proper emotions or respond appropriately to others from watching cartoons; they need warm, person-to-person interactions. The failure to form positive relationships with peers inflicts long-term socio-emotional consequences (Szewczyk-Sokolowski et al., 2005).

The human brain "downloads" the environment indiscriminately in an attempt to understand and absorb the surrounding world, whether that world is positive or negative. When children gain a sense of mastery of their environments, they are more likely to develop feelings of self-worth, confidence, and independence, which play heavily into the formation of children's personalities (Sroufe, 2005) and ultimately predict their success and happiness in relationships and in life in general. Economic hardship makes it more difficult for caregivers to create the trusting environments that build children's secure attachments. Behavior research shows that children from impoverished homes develop psychiatric disturbances and maladaptive social functioning at a greater rate than their affluent counterparts do (McCoy, Firck, Loney, & Ellis, 1999). In addition, low-SES children are more likely to have social conduct problems, as rated by both teachers and peers over a period of four years (Dodge, Pettit, & Bates, 1994). Unfortunately, a study of negative emotionality and maternal support found that low-income parents were less able than were well-off parents to adjust their parenting to the demands of higher-needs children (Paulussen-Hoogeboom, Stams, Hermanns, & Peetsma, 2007).

Low-income parents are often overwhelmed by diminished self-esteem, depression, and a sense of powerlessness and inability to cope—feelings that may get passed along to their children in the form of insufficient nurturing, negativity, and a general failure to focus on children's needs. In a study of emotional problems of children of single mothers, Keegan-Eamon and Zuehl (2001) found that the stress of poverty increases depression rates among mothers, which results in an increased use of physical punishment. Children themselves are also susceptible to depression: research shows that poverty is a major predictor of teenage depression (Denny, Clark, Fleming, & Wall, 2004).

Effects on School Behavior and Performance

Strong, secure relationships help stabilize children's behavior and provide the core guidance needed to build lifelong social skills. Children who grow up with such relationships learn healthy, appropriate emotional responses to everyday situations. But children raised in poor households often fail to learn these responses, to the detriment of their school performance. For example, students with emotional dysregulation may get so easily frustrated that they give up on a task when success was just moments away. And social dysfunction may inhibit students' ability to work well in cooperative groups, quite possibly leading to their exclusion by group members who believe they aren't "doing their part" or "pulling their share of the load." This exclusion and the accompanying decrease in collaboration and exchange of information exacerbate at-risk students' already shaky academic performance and behavior.

Some teachers may interpret students' emotional and social deficits as a lack of respect or manners, but it is more accurate and helpful to understand that the students come to school with a narrower range of appropriate emotional responses than we expect. The truth is that many children simply don't have the repertoire of necessary responses. It is as though their brains' "emotional keyboards" play only a few notes (see Figure 2.1).

The proper way to deal with such a deficit is first to understand students' behavior and then to lay out clear behavioral expectations without sarcasm

2.1 The Emotional Keyboard

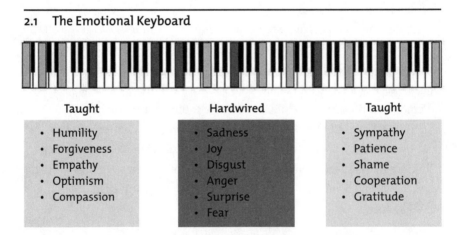

Taught	Hardwired	Taught
• Humility	• Sadness	• Sympathy
• Forgiveness	• Joy	• Patience
• Empathy	• Disgust	• Shame
• Optimism	• Anger	• Cooperation
• Compassion	• Surprise	• Gratitude
	• Fear	

The emotional brain can be represented by a keyboard on which children from poverty use fewer keys than well-off children. The six responses represented by the darker shading on the keyboard and in the center box are hardwired in our DNA. The responses represented by the lighter shading must be taught.

or resentment. Understand that children raised in poverty are more likely to display

- "Acting-out" behaviors.
- Impatience and impulsivity.
- Gaps in politeness and social graces.
- A more limited range of behavioral responses.
- Inappropriate emotional responses.
- Less empathy for others' misfortunes.

These behaviors will likely puzzle, frustrate, or irritate teachers who have less experience teaching students raised in poverty, but it's important to avoid labeling, demeaning, or blaming students. It is much easier to condemn a student's behavior and demand that he or she change it than it is to *help* the student change it. Every proper response that you don't see at your school is one that you need to be teaching. Rather than telling kids to "be respectful," demonstrate appropriate emotional responses and the circumstances in which to use them, and allow students to practice applying them. To shift your own responses to inappropriate behavior, reframe your thinking: *expect* students to be impulsive, to blurt inappropriate language, and to act "disrespectful" until you teach them stronger social and emotional skills and until the social conditions at your school make it attractive *not* to do those things.

It's impossible to overemphasize this: every emotional response other than the six hardwired emotions of joy, anger, surprise, disgust, sadness, and fear *must be taught.* Cooperation, patience, embarrassment, empathy, gratitude, and forgiveness are crucial to a smoothly running complex social environment (like a classroom). When students lack these learned responses, teachers who expect humility or penitence may get a smirk instead, a response that may lead teachers to believe the student has an "attitude." It's the primary caregiver's job to teach the child when and how to display these emotional responses, but when students do not bring these necessary behaviors to school, the school must teach them.

What all students *do* bring to school are three strong "relational" forces that drive their school behaviors (Harris, 2006):

1. **The drive for reliable relationships.** Students want the safety of a primary safe and reliable relationship. Students would prefer parents, positive friends, and teachers, but they'd take an "iffy" friend if no one else were available. The relationships that teachers build with students form the single strongest access to student goals, socialization, motivation, and academic performance. For your school to foster high achievement, every student will need a reliable partner or mentor.

2. **The strengthening of peer socialization.** Socialization is the drive for acceptance that encourages students to imitate their peers and join groups, from clubs to cliques to gangs. Students want to belong *somewhere*. Evidence suggests that it is peers, not parents, who have the greatest influence on school-age students (Harris, 1998). If your school aims to improve student achievement, academic success must be culturally acceptable among your students.

3. **The quest for importance and social status.** This is the quest to feel special. Students compete for attention and social elevation by choosing roles that will distinguish them (e.g., athlete, comedian, storyteller, gang leader, scholar, or style maverick). Kids are very interested in what other kids do, whether others like them, and how they rate on the social scale (Harris, 2006). Every student will need to feel like the "status hunt" can just as well lead to better grades as better behaviors.

Each of these forces shapes behaviors in significant ways. Schools that succeed use a combination of formal and informal strategies to influence these three domains. Informally, teachers can incorporate classroom strategies that build relationships and strengthen peer acceptance and social skills in class. This is a fair warning to all administrators: do not dismiss the so-called "soft side" of students' lives, the social side. It runs their brains, their feelings, and their behaviors—and those three run cognition! There is a complex interplay between cognition and emotions. When students feel socialized and accepted, they perform better academically. However, pushing students harder and harder into performing well academically may conflict with social/relational success. You will hit a test score ceiling until you include students' emotional and social lives in your school "makeover." Accordingly, throughout the remainder of this book, I offer specific strategies that address all three of the relational forces.

Action Steps

Embody respect. You can't change what's in your students' bank account, but you *can* change what's in their emotional account. It may require a considerable shift in your thinking. It is fruitless simply to demand respect from students; many just don't have the context, background, or skills to show it. Instead,

- Give respect to students first, even when they seem least to deserve it.
- Share the decision making in class. For example, ask students whether they would prefer to do a quick review of what they have learned to consolidate and strengthen their learning or move on to new material.
- Avoid such directives as "Do this right now!" Instead, maintain expectations while offering choice and soliciting input (e.g., "Would you rather do your rough draft now or gather some more ideas first?").
- Avoid demeaning sarcasm (e.g., "How about you actually do your assignment quietly for a change?").
- Model the process of adult thinking. For example, say, "We have to get this done first because we have only enough time for these three things today." Keep your voice calm and avoid labeling actions.
- Discipline through positive relationships, not by exerting power or authority. Avoid such negative directives as "Don't be a wise guy!" or "Sit down immediately!" Instead say, "We've got lots to do in class today. When you're ready to learn, please have a seat."

Embed social skills. At every grade level, use a variety of classroom strategies that strengthen social and emotional skills. For example,

- Teach basic but crucial meet-and-greet skills. Early in the year, when students introduce themselves to other classmates, teach students to face one another, make eye contact, smile, and shake hands.
- Embed turn-taking skills in class, even at the secondary level. You can introduce and embed these skills using such strategies as learning stations, partner work, and cooperative learning.
- Remind students to thank their classmates after completing collaborative activities.

- Implement social-emotional skill-building programs in the early years. Programs like the PATHS program, Conscious Discipline, and Love and Logic embed social skills into a classroom management framework.

Be inclusive. Create a familial atmosphere by using inclusive and affiliative language. For example,

- Always refer to the school as "our school" and the class as "our class"; avoid using a me-and-you model that reinforces power structures.
- Acknowledge students who make it to class, and thank them for small things.
- Celebrate effort as well as achievement; praise students for reaching milestones as well as for fulfilling end goals. Pack acknowledgments and celebrations into every single class.

Acute and Chronic Stressors

Stress can be defined as the physiological response to the perception of loss of control resulting from an adverse situation or person. Occasional or "roller-coaster" stress is healthy for all of us; it supports our immune function and helps develop resiliency. However, the acute and chronic stress that children raised in poverty experience leaves a devastating imprint on their lives. *Acute* stress refers to severe stress resulting from exposure to such trauma as abuse or violence, whereas *chronic* stress refers to high stress sustained over time. Low-SES children are more subject to both of these types of stress than are their more affluent peers, but chronic stress is more common and exerts a more relentless influence on children's day-to-day lives. Children living in poverty experience significantly greater chronic stress than do their more affluent counterparts (Almeida, Neupert, Banks, & Serido, 2005) (see Figure 2.2). This kind of stress exerts a devastating, insidious influence on children's physical, psychological, emotional, and cognitive functioning—areas that affect brain development, academic success, and social competence. Students subjected to such stress may lack crucial coping skills and experience significant behavioral and academic problems in school.

2.2   Number of Stressors for Poor vs. Nonpoor Children

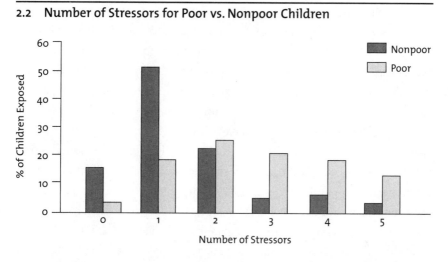

Source: Adapted from "Cumulative Risk, Maternal Responsiveness, and Allostatic Load Among Young Adolescents," by G. W. Evans, P. Kim, A. H. Ting, H. B. Tesher, and D. Shannis, 2007, *Developmental Psychology, 43*(2), pp. 341–351.

Theory and Research

The biology of stress is simple in some ways and complex in others. On a basic level, every one of the 30–50 trillion cells in your body is experiencing either healthy or unhealthy growth. Cells cannot grow and deteriorate at the same time. Ideally, the body is in homeostatic balance: a state in which the vital measures of human function—heart rate, blood pressure, blood sugar, and so on—are in their optimal ranges. A stressor is anything that threatens to disrupt homeostasis—for example, criticism, neglect, social exclusion, lack of enrichment, malnutrition, drug use, exposure to toxins, abuse, or trauma. When cells aren't growing, they're in a "hunker down" mode that conserves resources for a threatened future. When billions or trillions of cells are under siege in this manner, you get problems.

Although the body is well adapted to deal with short-term threats to homeostasis, chronic or acute stressors challenge the body differently. Among low-income families, stressors may include living in overcrowded, substandard housing or unsafe neighborhoods; enduring community or domestic violence, separation or divorce, or the loss of family members; and experiencing financial strain, forced mobility, or material deprivation (Evans & English, 2002). The frequency and intensity of both stressful life events and daily hassles are greater among low-SES children (Attar, Guerra, & Tolan, 1994). For example, in any given year, more than half of all poor children deal with evictions, utility disconnections, overcrowding, or lack of a stove or refrigerator, compared with only 13 percent of well-off children (Lichter, 1997). In addition, such factors as lack of proper supervision, physical neglect or abuse, inadequate day care and schools, difficulties in forming healthy friendships, and vulnerability to depression combine to exert inordinate and debilitating stress upon the developing child.

More often than not, low-income parents are overstressed in trying to meet the daily needs of their families. The resulting depression and negativity often lead to insufficient nurturing, disengaged parenting, and a difficulty in focusing on the needs of children. Compared with middle-income children, low-SES children are exposed to higher levels of familial violence, disruption, and separation (Emery & Laumann-Billings, 1998). Lower levels of parental education and occupation also correlate with greater incidence of neighborhood crimes (Sampson, Raudenbush, & Earls, 1997). And compared with their well-off peers, 2- to 4-year-olds from low-income families interact with aggressive peers 40 percent more often in their neighborhoods and 25 percent more often in child care settings (Sinclair, Pettit, Harrist, Dodge, & Bates, 1994).

Abuse is a major stressor to children raised in poverty. Numerous studies (Gershoff, 2002; Slack, Holl, McDaniel, Yoo, & Bolger, 2004) document that caregivers' disciplinary strategies grow harsher as income decreases. Lower-income parents are, on average, more authoritarian with their children, tending to issue harsh demands and inflict physical punishment such as spanking (Bradley, Corwyn, Burchinal, McAdoo, & Coll, 2001; Bradley, Corwyn, McAdoo, & Coll, 2001). One study found that blue-collar parents were twice as likely to use physical punishment with their 7-year-olds as white-collar parents were (Evans, 2004). Hussey, Chang, and Kotch (2006) found that poor children were 1.52 times more likely to report physical neglect and 1.83 times more likely to report sexual abuse than were well-off children. Abuse occurs with much higher frequency when the parents use alcohol or drugs, experience an array of stressful life events (Emery & Laumann-Billings, 1998), or live in decrepit, crime-ridden neighborhoods with limited social support networks (Jack & Jordan, 1999).

The cost of these constant stressors is hard to quantify. Exposure to chronic or acute stress is hardwired into children's developing brains, creating a devastating, cumulative effect (Coplan et al., 1996). Compared with a healthy neuron, a stressed neuron generates a weaker signal, handles less blood flow, processes less oxygen, and extends fewer connective branches to nearby cells. The prefrontal cortex and the hippocampus, crucial for learning, cognition, and working memory, are the areas of the brain most affected by *cortisol*, the so-called "stress hormone." Experiments have demonstrated that exposure to chronic or acute stress actually shrinks neurons in the brain's frontal lobes—an area that includes the prefrontal cortex and is responsible for such functions as making judgments, planning, and regulating impulsivity (Cook & Wellman, 2004)—and can modify and impair the hippocampus in ways that reduce learning capacity (Vythilingam et al., 2002).

Unpredictable stressors severely impair the brain's capacity to learn and remember (Yang et al., 2003). Child abuse, for example, is highly disruptive to such developmental processes as the formation of healthy attachments, emotional regulation, and temperament formation, and leads to a wide array of social-emotional and psychological disturbances in adulthood (Emery & Laumann-Billings, 1998). Neurobiological studies have shown considerable alterations in the brain development of neglected or abused children. The production of "fight-or-flight" stress hormones in these children atrophies the areas that control emotional regulation, empathy, social functioning, and other skills imperative to healthy emotional development (Joseph, 1999).

Chronic stress not only diminishes the complexity of neurons in the frontal lobe and the hippocampus but also increases the complexity of neurons in the amygdala, the brain's emotion center (Conrad, 2006). This increased complexity may make the stressed brain's neurons far more sensitive to memory modulation than neurons in nonstressed brains. In chronically stressed kids, the combined effects on the hippocampus and the amygdala may be precisely what facilitates *emotional* memory (the aspect of memory that encompasses highly salient memories of events such as divorce, abuse, trauma, death, or abandonment) and reduces *declarative* memory (the aspect of memory that stores standard knowledge and learning).

Chronic, unmediated stress often results in a condition known as an *allostatic load*. Allostatic load is "carryover" stress. Instead of returning to a healthy baseline of homeostasis, the growing brain adapts to negative life experiences so that it becomes either hyper-responsive or hypo-responsive. Szanton, Gill, and Allen (2005) found higher rates of chronic stress and allostatic load among low-income populations than among high-income populations.

Effects on School Behavior and Performance

Kids coming to your school don't wear signs that say "Caution! Chronic Stressors Live Here." But stress has an insidious effect on learning and behavior, and you should recognize the symptoms in the classroom. Chronic stress

- Is linked to over 50 percent of all absences (Johnston-Brooks, Lewis, Evans, & Whalen, 1998).
- Impairs attention and concentration (Erickson, Drevets, & Schulkin, 2003).
- Reduces cognition, creativity, and memory (Lupien, King, Meaney, & McEwen, 2001).
- Diminishes social skills and social judgment (Wommack & Delville, 2004).
- Reduces motivation, determination, and effort (Johnson, 1981).
- Increases the likelihood of depression (Hammack, Robinson, Crawford, & Li, 2004).
- Reduces neurogenesis (growth of new brain cells) (De Bellis et al., 2001).

A child who comes from a stressful home environment tends to channel that stress into disruptive behavior at school and be less able to develop a healthy social and academic life (Bradley & Corwyn, 2002). Impulsivity, for example, is a common disruptive classroom behavior among low-SES students. But it's actually an exaggerated response to stress that serves as a survival mechanism: in conditions of poverty, those most likely to survive are those who have an exaggerated stress response. Each risk factor in a student's life increases impulsivity and diminishes his or her capacity to defer gratification (see Figure 2.3) (Evans, 2003).

Students raised in poverty are especially subject to stressors that undermine school behavior and performance. For example, girls exposed to abuse tend to experience mood swings in school, while boys experience impairments in curiosity, learning, and memory (Zuena et al., 2008). And the stress resulting from transience—frequent short-distance, poverty-related moves (Schafft, 2006)—also impairs students' ability to succeed in school and engage in positive social interactions. Whereas middle-class families usually move for social or economic improvement, the moves of low-income households are typically not voluntary. In addition to increasing children's uncertainty about the future, these moves compound their stress load by disrupting their social interactions both within the community and in academic environments (Schafft, 2006).

2.3   Cumulative Risk Factors: More Stress = Less Delayed Gratification = More Impulsivity

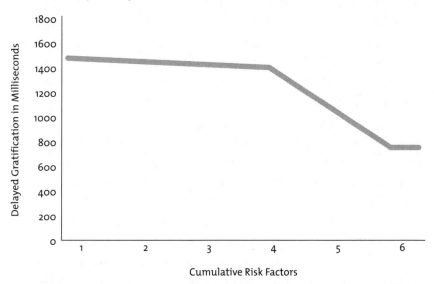

Source: Adapted from "A Multimethodological Analysis of Cumulative Risk and Allostatic Load Among Rural Children," by G. W. Evans, 2003, *Developmental Psychology, 39*(5), pp. 924–933.

Students who have to worry over safety concerns also tend to underperform academically (Pratt, Tallis, & Eysenck, 1997). Exposure to community violence—an unsafe home neighborhood or a dangerous path to school—contributes to lower academic performance (Schwartz & Gorman, 2003). In addition, stress resulting from bullying and school violence impairs test scores, diminishes attention spans, and increases absenteeism and tardiness (Hoffman, 1996). It is discouraging, but many high school students either stay home or skip classes due to fear of violence.

Socioeconomic status correlates positively with good parenting, which, research has found, improves academic achievement (DeGarmo, Forgatch, & Martinez, 1999). Unfortunately, the converse is also true: the chronic stress of poverty impairs parenting skills, and disengaged or negative parenting in turn impairs children's school performance. Parents who are struggling just to stay afloat tend to work extra hours, odd shifts, or multiple jobs and are less able to provide attention and affection and to devote their time, energy, and resources to their children. These deficits have been associated with higher levels of externalizing behaviors and poor academic performance on children's part (Hsuch & Yoshikawa, 2007).

Fishbein and colleagues (2006) found that adolescence, a period accompanied by dramatic brain changes, is a particularly vulnerable time for children to be exposed to chronic stress. They found that risky decision making (such as alcohol or drug use) and poor social competency correlated with adolescents' previous exposure to highly stressful life events.

In addition, stress adversely affects cognition. One randomized, double-blind, placebo-controlled study tested the effects of oral doses of cortisol (the stress chemical) on subjects (Newcomer et al., 1999). Cortisol treatment at the higher dose produced reversible decreases in verbal declarative memory in otherwise healthy individuals (Newcomer et al., 1999).

Exposure to chronic or acute stress is debilitating. The most common adaptive behaviors include increased anxiety (as manifested in generalized anxiety disorders or posttraumatic stress disorder) and an increased sense of detachment and helplessness. Students from low-income families who experience disruptive or traumatic events or who lack a measure of connectedness—to family, to the community, or to a religious affiliation—demonstrate increased hopelessness over time (Bolland, Lian, & Formichella, 2005). Nearly half

(47 percent) of low-SES African American adolescents reported clinically significant levels of depressive symptoms (Hammack et al., 2004). Low-SES students are more likely to give up or become passive and uninterested in school (Johnson, 1981). This giving-up process is known as *learned helplessness*. It's not genetic; it's an adaptive response to life conditions. And sadly, it frequently takes hold as early as 1st grade. Many kids with learned helplessness become fatalistic about their lives and are more likely to drop out of school or become pregnant while in their teens.

It is well documented that the effect of stressors is cumulative (Astone, Misra, & Lynch, 2007; Evans, 2004; Evans & English, 2002; Evans, Kim, Ting, Tesher, & Shannis, 2007; Geronimus, Hicken, Keene, & Bound, 2006; Lucey, 2007). Children who have had greater exposure to abuse, neglect, danger, loss, or other poverty-related experiences are more reactive to stressors. Each stressor builds on and exacerbates other stressors and slowly changes the student. It is the cumulative effect of all the stressors that often makes life miserable for poor students.

When researchers provided classes in appropriate coping skills and stress-relieving techniques, subjects demonstrated a decrease in hostility (Wadsworth, Raviv, Compas, & Connor-Smith, 2005) or depressive symptoms (Peden, Rayens, Hall, & Grant, 2005). Unfortunately, these interventions, along with stress-relieving recreational activities, are largely unavailable to those living in poverty. For example, neighborhood parks and recreational facilities tend to be scarcer, in hazardous areas, or in disrepair (Evans, 2004). Poor children are half as likely as well-off children are to be taken to museums, theaters, or the library, and they are less likely to go on vacations or on other fun or culturally enriching outings (Bradley & Corwyn, 2002).

Action Steps

Recognize the signs. Behavior that comes off as apathetic or rude may actually indicate feelings of hopelessness or despair. It is crucial for teachers to recognize the signs of chronic stress in students. Students who are at risk for a stress-related disorder tend to

- Believe that they have minimal control over stressors.
- Have no idea how long the stressors will last, or how intense they will remain.

- Have few outlets through which they can release the frustration caused by the stressors.
- Interpret stressors as evidence of circumstances worsening or becoming more hopeless.
- Lack social support for the duress caused by the stressors.

Share with other staff members why it's so important to avoid criticizing student impulsivity and "me first" behaviors. Whenever you and your colleagues witness a behavior you consider inappropriate, ask yourselves whether the discipline process is positive and therefore increases the chances for better future behavior, or whether it's punitive and therefore reduces the chances for better future behavior.

Alter the environment. Change the school environment to mitigate stress and resolve potential compliance issues with students who do not want to change:

- Reduce the parallels with prison. For example, consider eliminating bells and instead playing songs for class transitions.
- Reduce homework stress by incorporating time for homework in class or right after class.
- Use cooperative structures; avoid a top-down authoritarian approach.
- Help students blow off steam by incorporating celebrations, role-plays, and physical activities (e.g., walks, relays, or games) into your classes.
- Incorporate kinesthetic arts (e.g., drama or charades), creative projects (e.g., drawing or playing instruments), and hands-on activities (e.g., building or fixing) into your classes.

Empower students. Help students increase their perception of control over their environment by showing them how to better manage their own stress levels. Instead of telling students to act differently, take the time to teach them *how* to act differently by

- Introducing conflict resolution skills. For example, teach students a multistep process for handling upsets, starting with step 1: "Take a deep breath and count to five."
- Teaching students how to deal with anger and frustration (e.g., counting to 10 and taking slow, deep breaths).

- Introducing responsibilities and the value of giving restitution. In schools that embrace restitution, students understand that if they disrupt class, they need to "make it right" by doing something positive for the class. For example, a student who throws objects in the classroom may be assigned a cleaning or beautification project for the room.
- Teaching students to set goals to focus on what they want.
- Role-modeling how to solve real-world problems. Share an actual or hypothetical situation, such as your car running out of gas. You could explain that you tried to stretch the tank of gas too far and reveal how you dealt with the problem (e.g., calling a friend to bring some gas). Such examples show students how to take responsibility for and resolve the challenges they face in life.
- Giving students a weekly life problem to solve collectively.
- Teaching social skills. For example, before each social interaction (e.g., pair-share or buddy teaching), ask students to make eye contact, shake hands, and give a greeting. At the end of each interaction, have students thank their partners.
- Introducing stress reduction techniques, both physical (e.g., dance or yoga) and mental (e.g., guided periods of relaxation or meditation).

Cognitive Lags

Cognitive ability is highly complex. It can be measured in many different ways and is affected by numerous factors, not least of which is socioeconomic status. Socioeconomic status is strongly associated with a number of indices of children's cognitive ability, including IQ, achievement tests, grade retention rates, and literacy (Baydar, Brooks-Gunn, & Furstenberg, 1993; Brooks-Gunn, Guo, & Furstenberg, 1993; Liaw & Brooks-Gunn, 1994; Smith, Brooks-Gunn, & Klebanov, 1997). There is a gulf between poor and well-off children's performance on just about every measure of cognitive development, from the Bayley Infant Behavior Scales to standardized achievement tests. The correlations between socioeconomic status and cognitive ability and performance are typically quite significant (Gottfried, Gottfried, Bathurst, Guerin, & Parramore, 2003) and persist throughout the stages of development, from infancy through adolescence and into

2.4   How Experience Affects Cognitive Development

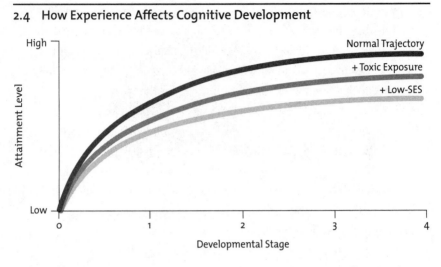

Source: Adapted from "Environmental Risk Factors in Infancy," by A. Sameroff, 1998, *Pediatrics, 102*(5), pp. 1287–1292.

adulthood (see Figure 2.4). But these are data, not destiny. The good news is that brains are designed to change.

Theory and Research

To function at school, the brain uses an overarching "operating system" that comprises a collection of neurocognitive systems enabling students to pay attention, work hard, process and sequence content, and think critically (see Figure 2.5). Five key systems are

• **The prefrontal/executive system.** This system, which engages the prefrontal cortex, includes our capacity to defer gratification, create plans, make decisions, and hold thoughts in mind. It also allows us to "reset" our brains' rules for how to behave. For example, we might have one set of rules for how to behave to our families and another set of rules for how to respond to strangers.

• **The left perisylvian/language system.** This system, which engages the temporal and frontal areas of the left brain hemisphere, encompasses semantic, syntactic, and phonological aspects of language. It is the foundation for our reading, pronunciation, spelling, and writing skills.

2.5 Brain Areas of Known Difference Between Low- and Middle-Income Children

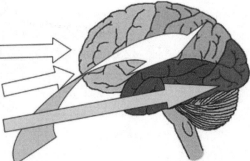

These areas include those responsible for working memory, impulse regulation, visuospatial skills, language skills, and cognitive conflict.

Source: Adapted from "Neurocognitive Correlates of Socioeconomic Status in Kindergarten Children," by K. G. Noble, M. F. Norman, and M. J. Farah, 2005, *Developmental Science, 8,* pp. 74–87.

- **The medial temporal/memory system.** This system allows us to process explicit learning (text, spoken words, and pictures) and, if appropriate, store that learning. It includes our "indexing" structure (the hippocampus) and our emotional processor (the amygdala).
- **The parietal/spatial cognition system.** This system underlies our ability to mentally represent and manipulate the spatial relations among objects and primarily engages the posterior parietal cortex. This brain area is especially important for organizing, sequencing, and visualizing information. It is essential for mathematics and music and for feeling a sense of organization.
- **The occipitotemporal/visual cognition system.** This system is responsible for pattern recognition and visual mental imagery, translating mental images into more abstract representations of object shape and identity, and reciprocally translating visual memory knowledge into mental images (Gardini, Cornoldi, De Beni, & Venneri, 2008).

The value of understanding "where" in the brain vital processes occur cannot be overstated; there are significant contrasts in these key systems between the brains of lower-SES and higher-SES individuals.

With the advent of cognitive neuroscience, it has become possible to assess these systems more selectively. One study (Noble, Norman, & Farah, 2005) examined the neurocognitive performance of 30 low-SES and 30 well-off African American kindergartners in the Philadelphia public schools. The children were tested on a battery of tasks adapted from the cognitive neuroscience literature, designed to assess the functioning of the aforementioned key neurocognitive systems. This was one of the first studies that showed both global and specific brain differences between lower-income and higher-income children. Another study (Farah et al., 2006) assessed middle schoolers' working memory and cognitive control and also found significant disparities between lower-income and higher-income students in the five neurocognitive areas. I'm often asked, "Has anyone actually scanned the brains of low-SES children and contrasted them with those of higher-SES children?" Yes, it has been done. And when the data are compiled and viewed by effect size, the areas of difference become dramatic (see Figure 2.6).

2.6   How Do the Brains of Children from Poverty Differ?

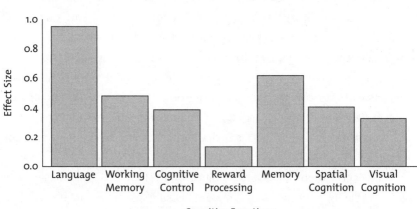

Note: Effect-size differences are measured in standard deviations of separation between low- and middle-income 5-year-olds.

Source: Adapted from "Neurocognitive Correlates of Socioeconomic Status in Kindergarten Children," by K. G. Noble, M. F. Norman, and M. J. Farah, 2005, *Developmental Science, 8*, pp. 74–87.

In another study (Noble, McCandliss, & Farah, 2007), 150 healthy, socioeconomically diverse 1st graders were administered tasks tapping language skills, visual-spatial skills, memory, working memory, cognitive control, and reward processing. Socioeconomic status accounted for more than 30 percent of the variance in the left perisylvian/language system and a smaller but significant portion of the variance in most other systems.

One possible explanation of the strong association between socioeconomic status and language is that the perisylvian brain regions involved in language processing undergo a more protracted course of maturation in vivo (i.e., once the child is born) than any other neural region (Sowell et al., 2003). It is possible that a longer period of development leaves the language system more susceptible to environmental influences (Noble et al., 2005).

For example, we have discovered that the quantity, quality, and context of parents' speech matter a great deal (Hoff, 2003). Children's vocabulary competence is influenced by the mother's socio-demographic characteristics, personal characteristics, vocabulary, and knowledge of child development (Bornstein, Haynes, & Painter, 1998). By the time most children start school, they will have been exposed to 5 million words and should know about 13,000 of them. By high school, they should know about 60,000 to 100,000 words (Huttenlocher, 1998). But that doesn't often happen in low-income homes. Weizman and Snow (2001) found that low-income caregivers speak in shorter, more grammatically simple sentences. There is less back-and-forth—fewer questions asked and fewer explanations given. As a result, children raised in poverty experience a more limited range of language capabilities. Figures 2.7 and 2.8 illustrate how parents' speech affects their children's vocabulary.

At the preschool level, inattention from care providers has a huge impact on the child's developing language skills and future IQ scores. A six-year study by Hart and Risley (1995) that followed the outcomes of children selected from different socioeconomic backgrounds found that by age 3, the children of professional parents were adding words to their vocabularies at about twice the rate of children in welfare families. Both the quantity and the quality of phrases directed at the children by caregivers correlated directly with income levels. They found that a pattern of slow vocabulary

2.7 Talking to Infants: The Cumulative Effects of Mother's Speech on Vocabulary of 2-Year-Olds

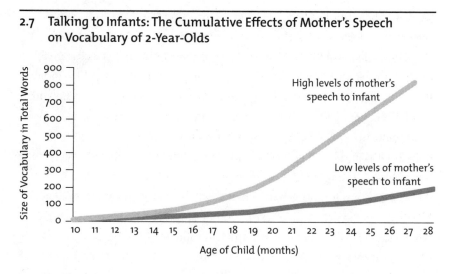

Source: Adapted from "Early Vocabulary Growth: Relation to Language Input and Gender," by J. Huttenlocher, W. Haight, A. Bryk, M. Seltzer, and R. Lyons, 1991, *Developmental Psychology,* 27(2), pp. 236–248.

2.8 Daily Parent-Child Speech Interactions

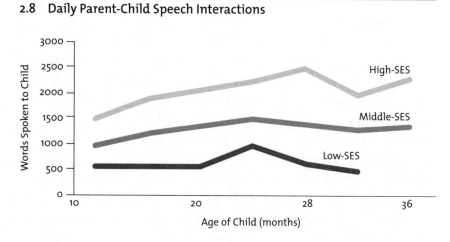

Source: Adapted from *Meaningful Differences in the Everyday Experiences of Young American Children,* by B. Hart and T. Risley, 1995, Baltimore: Brookes Publishing.

growth helped put in place a slower cognitive pattern by the time children turned 3. In fact, IQ tests performed later in childhood showed the welfare students' scores trailing behind those of the more affluent children by up to 29 percent. Parents of low socioeconomic status are also less likely to tailor their conversations to evoke thoughtful and reasoned responses from their children.

Going hand in hand with language acquisition, reading is one of the most important factors affecting the development of a child's brain. Reading skills are not hardwired into the human brain; every subskill of reading, including (but not limited to) phonological awareness, fluency, vocabulary, phonics, and comprehension, must be explicitly taught. This teaching requires attention, focus, and motivation from the primary caregiver. Again, the time and expertise to make this happen are unfortunately in short supply among poor families. Evidence suggests that poverty adversely alters the trajectory of the developing reading brain (Noble, Wolmetz, Ochs, Farah, & McCandliss, 2006).

Even when low-income parents do everything they can for their children, their limited resources put kids at a huge disadvantage. The growing human brain desperately needs coherent, novel, challenging input, or it will scale back its growth trajectory. When a child is neglected, the brain does not grow as much (De Bellis, 2005; Grassi-Oliveira, Ashy, & Stein, 2008). Unfortunately, low-SES children overall receive less cognitive stimulation than middle-income children do. For example, they are less likely to be read to by parents: Coley (2002) found that only 36 percent of low-income parents read to their kindergarten-age children each day, compared with 62 percent of upper-income parents. In addition, low-SES children are less likely to be coached in learning skills or helped with homework, and they are half as likely as their well-off peers to be taken to museums (Bradley, Corwyn, Burchinal et al., 2001; Bradley, Corwyn, McAdoo et al., 2001) and on other culturally enriching outings. They also have fewer play areas in their homes; have less access to computers and the Internet (and use them in less sophisticated ways); own fewer books, toys, and other recreational or learning materials; spend more time watching television; and are less likely to have friends over to play (Evans, 2004). Low-income parents' financial limitations often exclude their kids from healthy after-school activities, such as music, athletics, dance, or drama (Bracey, 2006).

Effects on School Behavior and Performance

Many children raised in poverty enter school a step behind their well-off peers. The cognitive stimulation parents provide in the early childhood years is crucial, and as we have seen, poor children receive less of it than their well-off peers do. These deficits have been linked to underdeveloped cognitive, social, and emotional competence in later childhood and have been shown to be increasingly important influences on vocabulary growth, IQ, and social skills (Bradley, Corwyn, Burchinal et al., 2001; Bradley, Corwyn, McAdoo et al., 2001). Standardized intelligence tests show a correlation between poverty and lower cognitive achievement, and low-SES kids often earn below-average scores in reading, math, and science and demonstrate poor writing skills. Although the effects of poverty are not automatic or fixed, they often set in motion a vicious and stubborn cycle of low expectations. Poor academic performance often leads to diminished expectations, which spread across the board and undermine children's overall self-esteem.

The dramatic socioeconomic divide in education doesn't help matters. High-poverty, high-minority schools receive significantly less state and local money than do more prosperous schools, and students in such schools are more likely to be taught by teachers who are inexperienced or teaching outside their specialties (Jerald, 2001) (see Figure 2.9). This gap is most evident in the subjects of math and reading.

2.9 Percentage of Teachers Outside Their Subject Expertise Assigned to Teach in High-Poverty Schools

	Math	English	History	Physical Science
All Public Schools	35.8%	33.1%	58.5%	59.1%
High-Poverty Schools	51.4%	41.7%	61.2%	61.2%

Source: Adapted from *Dispelling the Myth Revisited: Preliminary Findings from a Nationwide Analysis of "High-Flying" Schools,* by C. D. Jerald, 2001, Washington, DC: The Education Trust.

Constantino (2005) examined six communities in the greater Los Angeles, California, area and found that children in high-income communities had access to significantly more books than children in low-income communities did. In fact, she found that in some affluent communities, children had more books in their homes than low-SES children had in all school sources combined. Milne and Plourde (2006) identified six 2nd graders who came from low-income households but demonstrated high achievement and found that these children's parents provided educational materials, implemented and engaged in structured reading and study time, limited television viewing, and emphasized the importance of education. The researchers concluded that many of the factors of low socioeconomic status that negatively affect student academic success could be overcome by better educating parents about these essential needs.

The composite of academic skills needed for school success is actually a short list. I have introduced these skills as chunks scattered throughout this chapter. In Chapter 3, I list them together as an aggregate of subskills I call the fundamental "operating system" for academic success.

Action Steps

Build core skills. When students underperform academically, teachers can use assessments as an initial roadmap to ascertain the range and depth of skill building they need. Of course, assessments don't measure every skill that students need to succeed in school. Those core skills include

- Attention and focus skills.
- Short- and long-term memory.
- Sequencing and processing skills.
- Problem-solving skills.
- Perseverance and ability to apply skills in the long term.
- Social skills.
- Hopefulness and self-esteem.

Once you determine which skills your students most need to hone, create a plan, find a program, and allocate the resources. Later in this book, I address the logistics of implementing an intervention program. Some of the most important skills teachers should foster are social skills and problem-solving skills. When schools teach kids the social skills to resist peer pressure, for example, students stay in school longer, do better academically, and get in less trouble (Wright, Nichols, Graber, Brooks-Gunn, & Botvin, 2004). It is also essential to explicitly teach and model problem-solving skills and provide feedback to students. Here's an example of an established problem-solving process you can post in the classroom:

1. Identify and define the problem.
2. Brainstorm solutions.
3. Evaluate each solution with a checklist or rubric.
4. Implement the selected solution.
5. Follow up and debrief on the results to learn.

In addition to posting a model, you can create simple case studies with real-world problems for students to solve. For example, "You are leaving a shopping mall with friends late at night. Your friend is supposed to do the driving. But as far as you can tell, he looks pretty wasted. You have to get home soon or you'll get in trouble. What do you do?"

Pinpoint assessments. Helping to improve students' cognitive abilities and academic performance takes more than just knowing that a student is behind in a given area. For example, with reading skills, you'll want to find out if the student's difficulty is rooted in

- A vision or a hearing problem.
- A tracking issue.
- A vocabulary deficit.
- A comprehension challenge.
- A phonemic awareness or phonics issue.
- A fluency problem.

Quality assessment is essential, but follow-through is even more important. Pinpointed assessments are crucial to determine areas of strength and weakness. For example, the Woodcock-Johnson III Diagnostic Reading Battery can reveal specific areas that need targeted practice.

Provide hope and support. Any student who feels "less than" cognitively is likely not only to struggle academically, but also to be susceptible to such secondary issues as acting out, getting bullied or becoming a bully, having lower self-esteem, or having feelings of depression or helplessness. Ensure that teachers build supportive relationships, provide positive guidance, foster hope and optimism, and take time for affirmation and celebration.

Although the cognitive deficits in children from low-income families can seem daunting, the strategies available today are far more targeted and effective than ever before. Kids from all over the United States can succeed with the right interventions. I discuss these further in Chapters 4 and 5.

Recruit and train the best staff you can. You cannot afford to let disadvantaged kids receive substandard teaching. A Boston Public Schools (1998) study of the effects of teachers found that in one academic year, the top third of teachers produced as much as six times the learning growth as the bottom third of teachers did. Tenth graders taught by the least effective teachers made almost no gains in reading and even lost ground in math. To find superior teachers, start asking around the district and at conferences, post ads for teachers who love kids and love challenges, and ask the existing good teachers at your school, "How do we keep you here?" Recruiting great teachers is never easy, but it is possible if you know how to appeal to them. Top teachers crave challenge and workplace flexibility and look for highly supportive administrators. They continually strive to upgrade their skills and knowledge by participating in staff development, attending out-of-town conferences, and seeking out printed materials or DVDs. Appeal to their values and specify what you can offer.

Health and Safety Issues

As we have seen, low-SES children are often subject to such health and safety issues as malnutrition, environmental hazards, and insufficient health care. Health and achievement overlap: every cell in our body needs a healthy environment to function optimally. When a body's cells are besieged daily by stressors, they slow their growth trajectory and contract. Kids raised in poverty have more cells in their body "under siege" than do kids from middle- or upper-income families. The consequent adaptations that these kids' immune systems make diminish their ability to concentrate, learn, and behave appropriately.

Theory and Research

Stanford neuroscientist and stress expert Robert Sapolsky (2005) found that the lower a child's socioeconomic status is, the lower his or her overall health. Substandard housing in low-income neighborhoods leaves children exposed to everything from greater pedestrian risks (heavier traffic on narrower streets) to environmental hazards (exposure to radon and carbon monoxide) (Evans, 2004). Poor housing quality may cause respiratory morbidity and childhood injuries (Matte & Jacobs, 2000) and may elevate psychological distress in children (Evans, Wells, & Moch, 2003). Poor children are more likely to live in old and inadequately maintained housing and to be exposed to lead in peeling paint (Sargent et al., 1995)—a factor associated with decreased IQ (Schwartz, 1994). And, as with other risk factors, these negative environmental effects synergize with and build on one another (Evans & Kantrowitz, 2002).

The lower parents' income is, the more likely it is that children will be born premature, low in birth weight, or with disabilities (Bradley & Corwyn, 2002). Expectant mothers living in poverty are more likely to live or work in hazardous environments; to be exposed to pesticides (Moses et al., 1993); and to smoke, drink alcohol, or use drugs during pregnancy, all factors linked to prenatal issues and birth defects (Bradley & Corwyn, 2002) and adverse cognitive outcomes in children (Chasnoff et al., 1998).

Children from low-income families have generally poorer physical health than do their more affluent peers. In particular, there is a higher incidence of such conditions as asthma (Gottlieb, Beiser, & O'Connor, 1995), respiratory infections (Simoes, 2003), tuberculosis (Rogers & Ginzberg, 1993), ear infections and hearing loss (Menyuk, 1980), and obesity (Wang & Zhang, 2006). Contributing factors include poor nutrition (Bridgman & Phillips, 1998), unhealthy environmental conditions, and inability to obtain appropriate health care. Children with no health insurance may receive little or no treatment for illnesses and are far more likely to die from injuries or infections than are well-off children (Bradley & Corwyn, 2002). In addition, early health conditions may have significant long-term consequences, even if children's socioeconomic status improves later in life (McLoyd, 1998). Further, Broadman (2004) found that a significant portion of health differentials across neighborhoods (high- and low-income) could be explained by the disparate levels of stress across these neighborhoods.

Effects on School Behavior and Performance

The greater incidence of health issues among lower-income students leads to increased

- School absences.
- Duration of school absences.
- Tardiness rates.
- Incidents of illness during class.
- Rates of undiagnosed and/or untreated health problems or disabilities.

Each of these issues can occur among middle- and upper-income students, but they are both more common and more severe among students living in poverty. As a result, low-SES kids are often missing key classroom content and skills. Teachers may see students as uncaring or uninterested, when the real issue is that they're not in class enough to keep up.

Action Steps

Increase health-related services. Lower-income students face a daunting array of health issues. Successful schools understand these challenges and provide wide-ranging support and accommodations. Such support may include

- Providing a physician on-site once a week.
- Working with a local pharmacy to arrange for access to medications.
- Arranging for a dentist to make designated school visits.
- Educating students' caregivers about school resources.
- Providing tutors to help students who miss classes to catch up.
- Improving awareness among staff about health-related issues.

There are serious limitations on what schools can and should do about student health. But all of us understand that when we don't feel right, it's hard to listen, concentrate, and learn. Successful schools find ways to ensure that students have a fighting chance to get and stay healthy.

Develop an enrichment counterattack. A compelling body of research (Dobrossy & Dunnett, 2004; Green, Melo, Christensen, Ngo, & Skene, 2006; Guilarte, Toscano, McGlothan, & Weaver, 2003; Nithianantharajah & Hannan, 2006) suggests that early exposure to toxins, maternal stress, trauma, alcohol, and other negatives can be ameliorated with environmental enrichment. The better the school environment is, the less the child's early risk factors will impair his or her academic success. An enrichment school

- Provides wraparound health and medical services.
- Minimizes negative stress and strengthens coping skills.
- Uses a cognitively challenging curriculum.
- Provides tutoring and pullout services to build student skills.
- Fosters close relationships with staff and peers.
- Offers plenty of exercise options.

The whole point of school ought to be to enrich the life of every student. Enrichment does not mean "more" or "faster" schooling. It means rich, balanced, sustained, positive, and contrasting learning environments. That's what will change students' lives over the long haul (see Figure 2.10).

Beating the Odds

This chapter has painted a bleak picture of children raised in poverty. Certainly not all children raised in poverty experience the brain and behavioral

---

2.10 Benefits of Academic Enrichment for Children from Poverty

Kindergarten to 21 Years Old

Increased
- Intelligence (IQ)
- Reading and Math Skills
- Academic Locus of Control
- Social Competence
- Years in School, Including College
- Full-Time Employment

Decreased
- Grade Repetition
- Special Education Placement
- Teen Pregnancy
- Smoking and Drug Use

Source: Adapted from "The Development of Cognitive and Academic Abilities: Growth Curves from an Early Childhood Educational Experiment," by F. A. Campbell, E. P. Pungello, S. Miller-Johnson, M. Burchinal, and C. T. Ramey, 2001, *Developmental Psychology, 37*(2), pp. 231–242.

changes described in this chapter, but we have seen that an aggregation of disadvantages creates a difficult web of negatives. Poverty penetrates deeper into the body, brain, and soul than many of us realize.

A childhood spent in poverty often sets the stage for a lifetime of setbacks. Secure attachments and stable environments, so vitally important to the social and emotional development of young children, are often denied to our neediest kids. These children experience more stress due to loneliness, aggression, isolation, and deviance in their peer relationships, and they are more likely to describe feeling deprived, embarrassed, picked on, or bullied. As a result, they more often face future struggles in marital and other relationships.

However, research (Hill, Bromell, Tyson, & Flint, 2007) suggests that although the first five years of a child's life are very important, there is tremendous opportunity during the school years for significant transformation. Low-SES children's behavior is an adaptive response to a chronic condition of poverty, but a brain that is susceptible to adverse environmental effects is equally susceptible to positive, enriching effects. You'll learn more about how brains can change for the better in Chapter 3.

3

Embracing the Mind-Set of Change

When Mr. Hawkins's more enthusiastic colleagues share how they have changed students' lives over the course of a year, he is skeptical. He doesn't see changes in his students. Years ago, he met the mother of one of his kids and observed that "the apple doesn't fall far from the tree." He has noticed how much Jason, one of his current students, behaves like his older brother, Kevin, who dropped out in 11th grade. In his 14 years of teaching experience, Mr. Hawkins has watched this cycle repeat itself over and over again. He continues to think about retirement, only six years away.

The Bad News and the Good News

We have established that the effects of poverty on the brain can be devastating. The good news is that being raised in poverty is not a sentence for a substandard life. Research suggests that how well and how quickly we help kids adapt to school forecasts long-term schooling outcomes (Stipek, 2001). When teachers express despair over working with low-SES kids, I tell them, "The reason things stay the same is because *we've* been the same. For things to change, *we* must change!" Brains are designed to reflect the environments they're in, not rise above them. If we want our students to change, we must change ourselves and the environments students spend time in every day. In this chapter, I address the questions "Can the brain change for the better?" and "How can we make it happen?"

Brains Can Change

Neuroplasticity and Gene Expression

The most crucial concept to keep in mind when working with any population of underachieving school-age kids is this: brains can and do change. Brains are *designed* to change. Some changes are gradual, like those resulting from learning a new language, while other changes are instant, like those resulting from "aha" moments. Some changes are positive, such as those wrought by quality nutrition, exercise, and learning; other changes are negative, such as those resulting from long-term neglect, chronic drug abuse, and boredom.

Relatively recently, we have learned that we can intentionally change the brain's structure and organization. *Neuroplasticity* is the quality that allows region-specific changes to occur in the brain as a result of experience. When the experience is narrow and specific, such as an accident resulting in head trauma, you get narrow, specific changes, whereas broader experiences—such as exercise or maturation—result in more global changes. Research has shown that our parietal, frontal, and temporal lobes are all receptive to specific stimuli that cause measurable neural changes. Here are some examples of experience-based brain changes:

- Video games may enhance players' attention skills (Dye, Green, & Bavelier, 2009).
- Intensive language training evokes measurable physical changes in auditory brain maps (Meinzer et al., 2004).
- With training, deaf people may develop enhanced visual capacity (Dye, Hauser, & Bavelier, 2008).
- Spatial navigation abilities may correlate with a larger-than-average hippocampus, an area responsible for explicit learning and memory (Maguire et al., 2003).
- Learning to play music may cause changes in several sensory, motor, and higher-order association areas of the brain that result in improved attention, sequencing, and processing (Stewart, 2008).
- Learning new skills may result in increases in brain processing speed and structural size (Driemeyer, Boyke, Gaser, Büchel, & May, 2008).

- During periods of intense learning, students may experience increases in gray matter of 1–3 percent in the areas of the brain most involved with their studies (Draganski et al., 2006).
- Chronic pain changes the brain (May, 2008). One study (Teutsch, Herken, Bingel, Schoell, & May, 2008) showed that repeated painful stimulation resulted in a substantial increase of gray matter in the areas of the brain involved with pain transmittal. These changes are stimulation-dependent (i.e., they recede after the pain input ends).

On every single day of school, your students' brains will be changing. When their brains change, so do their levels of attention, learning, and cognition. Whether they are changing for better or for worse depends heavily on the quality of the staff at your school.

The old debate pits genes versus environmental factors, or nature versus nurture. That debate is outdated. Today, we recognize a third factor: *gene expression*. Virtually unheard of 20 years ago, gene expression refers to the translation of information encoded in a gene into protein or RNA. This process "switches on" or activates the gene. Genes can be either active (expressed) or silent (not expressed). Think about it: all humans share over 99 percent of the same genes. Yet look at any two humans, and the shared genes may be expressed in one person and not in another. This factor is a huge source of differentiation among humans. It explains why family members—even identical twins—can share the same DNA and yet have very different personalities.

For example, variations in maternal care can alter the activity of the genes in children's brains, and this change in gene expression may alter how children respond to stress (Weaver et al., 2004). The study of these reversible heritable changes in gene function, or the capacity of environmental factors (e.g., stress, nutrition, exercise, learning, and socialization) to influence gene activity, is known as *epigenetics,* which I briefly touched on in Chapter 2. The new understandings that have emerged from this field have strong implications: educators must rethink old ideas that limit students' academic potential to their performance on an IQ test. Through gene expression, students can make significant transformations in behavior and cognition regardless of the genetic makeup of their parents.

Changing IQ

If brains can physically change, does this mean we can change one of the traditional measures of intelligence, IQ? Evidence (Gottfredson, 2004) suggests that many low-SES students begin school with a lower-than-average IQ. Are they academically "stuck," or can their IQs increase? There's good news. Intelligence (as measured by IQ tests), although highly inheritable, is not 100 percent genetically determined. Twin studies show us that a whopping 60 percent of the variance in IQ is attributable to epigenetic factors, such as socioeconomic status (Turkheimer, Haley, Waldron, D'Onofrio, & Gottesman, 2003). Research shows that IQ may also be affected by such factors as

- Home environment and living conditions (Tong, Baghurst, Vimpani, & McMichael, 2007).
- Early childhood experiences and early educational intervention (Chaudhari et al., 2005).
- Amount and duration of schooling (Cooper, Nye, Charlton, Lindsay, & Greathouse, 1996; Murray, 1997; Wahlsten, 1997; Winship & Korenman, 1997).
- Quality of nutrition (Isaacs et al., 2008).

These and other data indicate that IQ is not fixed but variable, and we can influence many of the factors influencing it. One way to test this theory is to identify adopted children with already-tested low IQs, enrich their living conditions, and then measure their IQs later, comparing them with a control group. One adoption study did precisely that.

Out of a large randomized sample pool of 5,003 files of adopted children, researchers (Duyme, Dumaret, & Tomkiewicz, 1999) identified 65 deprived children who were adopted between 4 and 6 years of age and had a pre-adoption IQ below 86. Due to abuse or neglect as infants, these children had an average IQ of 77. When tested again in early adolescence, the children's average IQ score was 91. (See Figure 3.1.) The lower a child's initial IQ was, the greater the gain; children who had low pre-adoption IQs earned much higher scores in adolescence (Duyme et al., 1999). Disadvantaged kids who were given enhanced conditions for eight years boosted their IQs by as much as 20 points! The adoptive parents tended to work as managers, tradesmen, or craftsmen; were more likely to speak with a higher-level

---

3.1   Environmental Change Raises IQ Scores in Low-SES Students

Sixty-five low-SES children were adopted at ages 4–6 (with IQ scores <86 before adoption). After 8 years, the average overall IQ gain was a significant 13.9 points, and 19.5 points when they were adopted by high-SES families.

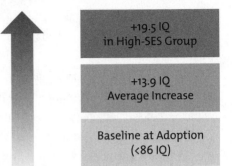

+19.5 IQ
in High-SES Group

+13.9 IQ
Average Increase

Baseline at Adoption
(<86 IQ)

Source: Adapted from "How Can We Boost IQs of 'Dull Children'? A Late Adoption Study," by M. Duyme, A.-C. Dumaret, and S. Tomkiewicz, 1999, *Proceedings of the National Academy of Sciences of the United States of America, 96*(15), pp. 8790–8794.

---

vocabulary; and were more likely to explore local museums and libraries and to travel to other countries. Capron and Duyme (1989) found that children born to *or* adopted by higher-income parents scored higher than lower-income *parents* did.

Let's approach the question from a slightly different angle. More than 50 years ago, researcher Harold Skeels wondered if retardation in young children could be reversed. He composed an experimental group of 13 children from an orphanage who were designated as mentally retarded and unsuitable for adoption, and transferred them to an institution for people with mental retardation. Then he arranged for each child to be a "house guest" on a ward—a bit like an inclusion classroom for students with disabilities. Each child had an affectionate caregiver as well as other "aunts" to connect to. At the same time, Skeels observed a comparison group of 12 orphanage infants who were not considered retarded. The experiment continued for three years (Skeels, 1966).

Two years after the end of the intervention, the experimental group had experienced an average gain of 29 IQ points, while the control group had experienced an average loss of 26 IQ points. Five years later, this trend was sustained, and a 30-year follow-up found that the median grade in school completed was 12.0 (graduation from high school) for the experimental group versus 2.75 (3rd grade) for the control group. All of the members of the experimental group were self-supporting, whereas most in the control group were dependent on others, with five still in institutions. Finally, the 28 children of the members of the experimental group (i.e., the next generation) had a mean IQ of 104! Environment clearly matters.

A number of randomized controlled trials have shown that educational intervention has the potential to narrow the performance gap across socioeconomic status. For instance, the IQ of low-SES children who have participated in intensive early education is between one-half and one full standard deviation higher than the IQ of children in low-income control groups (Ramey & Ramey, 1998). Although critics often conclude that the benefits of early intervention wane shortly after termination of the program (Haskins, 1989), some studies have shown effects that are sustained (Brooks-Gunn et al., 1994) and cost-effective (meaning the interventions can be replicated with available city and state funds and are not dependent on federal grants) (Barnett, 1998).

An as-yet-untested approach to maximizing the efficacy of interventions is to focus programs on the neurocognitive abilities that vary most steeply with socioeconomic status, including working memory, vocabulary, ability to defer gratification, self-control, and language skills. In addition, neurocognitive analysis may reveal the different mediating roles that various SES-related factors play across neurocognitive systems. By examining which underlying factors are associated with which cognitive abilities, we can design and test interventions with increased efficacy.

Although having a higher IQ does make a student more likely to stay in school, staying in school can itself either elevate IQ or prevent it from slipping. In fact, each additional month a student remains in school may increase his or her IQ above what it would have been had he or she dropped out. The earliest evidence comes from the turn of the last century, when the London Board of Education studied children who had very low IQ scores. The board's report revealed that the IQ of children in the same family decreased from the youngest to the oldest. The youngest children—ages 4 to 6—had an average IQ of 90, while the oldest children—ages 12 to 22— had an average IQ of only 60. This finding suggests that factors other than heredity are at work (Kanaya, Scullin, & Ceci, 2003): the older children progressively missed more school, and their IQs plummeted as a result.

IQ is affected by the amount of schooling students receive. Remaining in school longer has been shown to increase Wechsler IQ test scores. Here's an illustration. In 1970, toward the end of the Vietnam War, a U.S. draft priority was established by lottery. Men born on July 9, 1951, were picked first and thus tended to stay in school longer to avoid the draft, whereas men whose birthdays were matched with higher numbers had no incentive to stay in school longer because it was unlikely that they would be called for the draft. As a result, men born on July 9 not only had higher IQs but also earned approximately 7 percent more money than did men born on, say, July 7, who were picked last for the draft (Ceci, 2001). Students' Wechsler IQ scores are affected even by summer vacations: independent studies have documented that there is a systematic decline in IQ scores over the summer months (Cooper et al., 1996). The decline is most pronounced for children whose summers are least academically oriented.

Dropping out of school can also diminish IQ. One large-scale study (Ceci, 1991) randomly selected 10 percent of all males in the Swedish school population born in 1948 (numbering about 55,000) and administered an IQ test to these students at age 13. In 1966, 4,616 of the now-18-year-olds were tested again. For each year of high school not completed, students experienced an average loss of 1.8 IQ points (Murray, 1997). Evidence shows that each year of school a student misses can cause IQ to drop up to 5 points (Wahlsten, 1997), whereas remaining in school boosts IQ by an average of 2.7 points per year (Winship & Korenman, 1997).

Aside from these factors, a large body of research supports the existence of the *Flynn effect,* which describes the tendency of IQ scores to increase from one generation to the next (Flynn, 1984). Studies have observed this trend in a wide variety of samples and indicate that mean IQ scores tend to rise over time regardless of culture or race (Rushton, 2000) and even in samples of children labeled as learning disabled (Sanborn, Truscott, Phelps, & McDougal, 2003). In fact, mean IQs have increased more than 15 points—a full standard deviation—during the last 50 years worldwide (Bradmetz & Mathy, 2006). How? One speculation is that changes in technology have spawned a new generation with the exact skills that get rewarded on IQ tests.

Fluid Intelligence

As we have seen, a host of factors affects IQ. But we can change IQ even more directly and purposefully by fostering *fluid intelligence*—that is, students' ability to rapidly adjust their strategies and thought processes from one context to another. For example, a student who has learned the rule of looking both ways before crossing the street would be able to apply this learning in, say, the context of approaching a busy intersection. ("Maybe I should approach slowly; there seems to be a lot of construction going on.") Fluid intelligence generally encompasses problem solving, pattern recognition, and abstract thinking and reasoning skills, as well as the ability to draw inferences and understand the relationships of concepts outside the formal, specific instruction and practice related to those concepts.

Often, skill sets we learn in one context are not useful in other contexts. For example, one study found that adolescent street vendors in Brazil were quite capable of doing the math required for their role as sellers (98 percent accuracy), but many could not complete the *exact same problem* in a classroom context (56 percent accuracy) (Carraher, Carraher, & Schliemann, 1985). Similarly, another study found that female shoppers who had no difficulty comparing product values at the supermarket were unable to carry out the same mathematical operations on paper-and-pencil tests in a lab situation (Lave, 1988). Yet another study found that skilled handicappers were able to use a highly complex interactive model with as many as seven variables in wagering on harness races, but could not do this in a formal setting (Ceci & Liker, 1986). These subjects' "smarts" were contextual and nontransferable.

Fluid intelligence is a context-independent, highly transferable skill that will serve your students well in the real world. And if, as science suggests, the brain has plasticity, then we ought to be able to teach this crucial type of intelligence to students with lower IQ scores (see Figure 3.2).

The good news is that it *can* be taught; in fact, the more hours of training that students receive, the greater the effects are (Jaeggi, Buschkuehl, Jonides, & Perrig, 2008). Teachers can start by having students apply writing strategies like brainstorming, mind maps, and prewriting to other scenarios. Or for a science project, students could apply the stair-step planning process by using graphic organizers and setting objectives. To get you started, many

3.2   Fluid Intelligence Can Be Taught

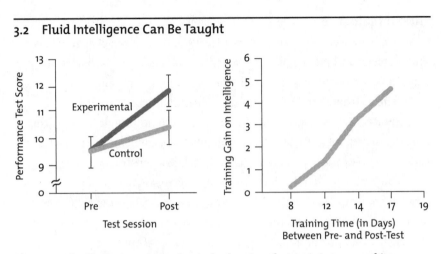

These graphs illustrate results of a study showing that training on working memory can improve students' fluid intelligence.

Source: Adapted from "Improving Fluid Intelligence with Training on Working Memory," by S. M. Jaeggi, M. Buschkuehl, J. Jonides, and W. J. Perrig, 2008, *Proceedings of the National Academy of Sciences of the United States of America, 105*(19), pp. 6829–6833.

Web sites offer fluid-intelligence builders, including www.soakyourhead.com and www.lumosity.com.

How We Can Change the Brain for the Better

We now know not only that students' brains can change but also that we can play a part in changing them. But it takes more than the will to do it; you also need the know-how.

Some schools try to make kids "smarter" by simply trying to stuff more curriculum into their brains. This strategy is not supported by science and typically backfires by making students feel overmatched or bored. Kids raised in poverty need more than just content; they need *capacity*. Is it possible to build a brain that's more capable, more flexible, and faster, with greater processing capacity?

A statistical strategy called multivariate analysis has helped us find that genetic influences within and among academic domains overlap a great deal (Kovas et al., 2007). This analysis showed that many of the same genes correlated with reading difficulties were also correlated with math difficulties—

for example, the ability to sort, sequence, and process data is used for both domains. Behavioral geneticist Robert Plomin's studies are of particular interest to those who want to change students' lives. His DNA research suggests the likelihood of "generalist genes" that serve multiple learning functions (Plomin & Kovas, 2005). We know that numerous epigenetic factors influence gene expression. Plomin observes, "If genetic effects on cognition are so general, the effects of these genes on the brain are also likely to be general. In this way, generalist genes may prove invaluable in integrating top-down and bottom-up approaches to the systems biology of the brain" (Davis et al., 2008). When you change the environment to help express your students' generalist genes, you get a broad, significant ripple effect on behavior and learning. But to get dramatic results, you must upgrade students' brains' "operating systems."

The Brain's Operating System

To succeed in school, students need to have an academic operating system in place (see Figure 3.3). This operating system does not include absolutely everything kids need in life; our brains develop other operating systems for socialization, survival, and work, for example. The academic operating system does not include such values as love, sacrifice, duty, fairness, humor, and kindness. But as far as school success goes, these are the must-haves:

- The ability and motivation to defer gratification and make a sustained effort to meet long-term goals.
- Auditory, visual, and tactile processing skills.
- Attentional skills that enable the student to engage, focus, and disengage as needed.
- Short-term and working memory capacity.
- Sequencing skills (knowing the order of a process).
- A champion's mind-set and confidence.

These skills form the foundation for school success and can give students the capacity to override the adverse risk factors of poverty. These are not simple study skills; they enable students to focus on, capture, process, evaluate, prioritize, manipulate, and apply or present information in a meaningful way. Without improving students' brains' capacity to process incoming data,

3.3   Academic Operating System

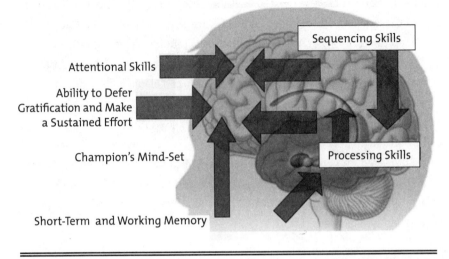

Sequencing Skills

Attentional Skills

Ability to Defer
Gratification and Make
a Sustained Effort

Champion's Mind-Set

Processing Skills

Short-Term and Working Memory

student achievement will stagnate. An old Commodore 64 computer had so little processing power that no matter how slowly you typed or how little content you had, the system still tended to get overwhelmed. To improve students' processing capacity, you must give them support as you challenge them. Every successful school intervention for low-SES kids features some variation on the theme of rebuilding the operating system and honing the fewest processes that matter most to the learning process. Such interventions *enrich* students. Enrichment can be described as the result of positive changes in an organism that arise from a sustained, positive contrast to the organism's prevailing impoverished environment.

The processes in the brain's academic operating system are malleable and can be trained and improved through a variety of activities. For example,

- Physical activity can increase the production of new brain cells (Pereira et al., 2007), a process highly correlated with learning, mood, and memory.
- Playing chess can increase students' capabilities in reading (Margulies, 1991) and math (Cage & Smith, 2000) by increasing attention, motivation, processing, and sequencing skills.
- The arts can improve attention, sequencing, processing, and cognitive skills (Gazzaniga, Asbury, & Rick, 2008).

• Completing tasks administered by computer-aided instructional programs that have subjects identify, count, and remember objects and hold those objects' locations in their working memories can increase attention and improve working memory within several weeks, even generalizing to improve performance on other memory tasks and an unrelated reasoning task (Kerns, Eso, & Thomson, 1999; Klingberg et al., 2005; Westerberg & Klingberg, 2007).

Music is a good example of a skill builder that can significantly improve students' academic operating systems. Music training enhances self-discipline, wide brain function, and verbal memory (Chan, Ho, & Cheung, 1998). It has been found to improve performance in the core mathematical system for representing abstract geometry, detecting geometric properties of visual forms, relating Euclidean distance to numerical magnitude, and using geometric relationships between forms on a map to locate objects in a larger spatial layout (Spelke, 2008). In addition, the rehearsal process develops focused attention, which in turn enhances memory (Jonides, 2008). Finally, music enhances students' long-term will and effort. It takes so long to reach proficiency that students learn the power of persistence, which is more strongly correlated with good grades than IQ itself is (Duckworth & Seligman, 2006).

These simple but dramatic illustrations are perfect examples of our capacity to escape our own genomes. Genes provide blueprints, but they are susceptible to environmental and social input. Nobel laureate Eric Kandel (1998) noted that "the regulation of gene expression by social factors makes all bodily functions, including all functions of the brain, susceptible to social influences. These social influences will be biologically incorporated in the altered expressions of specific genes in specific nerve cells of specific regions of the brain. These socially influenced alterations are transmitted culturally" (p. 461). Note the emphasis on cultural influence; we'll return to that theme in Chapter 4.

Most low-SES kids' brains have adapted to survive their circumstances, not to get As in school. Their brains may lack the attention, sequencing, and processing systems for successful learning. It's up to us to upgrade their operating systems—or see a downgrade in their performance.

Educational Intervention and Long-Term Enrichment

In an effort to maximize educational gains, educators and policymakers are placing more importance on the early education of the 19 million children in the United States under the age of 5. The first few years of life are crucial for a child's learning and cognitive development. The long-term benefits of high-quality early education programs are well documented (Campbell, Pungello, Miller-Johnson, Burchinal, & Ramey, 2001; Ramey & Ramey, 2006). Studies have shown that educational intervention has the potential to narrow or eliminate the socioeconomic performance gap, showing sustained (Brooks-Gunn et al., 1994) and cost-effective (Barnett, 1998) results. Evaluations of well-run prekindergarten programs have found that children exposed to high-quality early education were less likely to drop out of school, repeat grades, or need special education, compared with similar children who did not have such exposure (Barnett, 1998). Research into individual, early childhood, or school-based enrichment interventions has demonstrated that quality enrichment programs

- Improve language fluency, IQ, and other cognitive processes.
- Reduce school problems and academic failure in both elementary and high school.
- Improve social, academic, and emotional intelligence when implemented in early childhood (Campbell et al., 2001).

In addition, children in these programs display fewer risk behaviors, have fewer legal problems, are less likely to drop out of school, and are less dependent on welfare. Results are clearly linked to the quality and duration of interventions; smaller, customized, age-appropriate activities that continue over time are essential. Many improvements take four to six years (Campbell & Ramey, 1994). In some cases, enrichment may be very expensive, but the benefits can be long-lasting.

One key study (Williams et al., 2002) examined an intervention that developed the practical intelligence (i.e., intelligence that is directly actionable in everyday life) of middle school students from diverse socioeconomic backgrounds attending diverse types of schools and found that it boosted achievement. Students who develop practical intelligence are able to self-assess and self-correct during the learning process, instead of afterward.

Teachers in the study were trained to deliver a program emphasizing five sources of metacognitive awareness: *knowing why, knowing self, knowing differences, knowing process,* and *revisiting.* The thinking skills teachers taught enhanced students' practical and academic abilities in each of the target skill areas (reading, writing, homework, and test taking). Results indicated that thinking skills can be taught to enhance academic success: the researchers worked with teachers in Connecticut and Massachusetts schools over a two-year period and found that the children (all from diverse socioeconomic backgrounds) experienced increased outcomes in the four skill areas (Williams et al., 2002).

The Boys & Girls Clubs of America put together an enriching after-school program designed to help low-SES students living in public housing. The program was set up outside school, close to kids' homes, and provided transportation and met parental wishes in terms of time of day, cost, transportation, and curriculum. Follow-up data (Schinke, Cole, & Poulin, 2000) gave strong statistical support to the provision of educational enhancements in nonschool settings for at-risk youths. These data, collected 30 months after the program started, showed

- Improved reading, verbal, writing, and tutoring skills.
- Better overall school performance.
- Stronger interest in class material.
- Higher school grades than those of the control group.
- Improved school attendance

Environmental enrichment programs can be very effective in changing the IQs of children living in low-SES families. Many researchers think that the earlier the interventions the better, because there may be a "sensitive" time for the brain, from birth to age 5, when it is more receptive to major rewiring. Yet there is tremendous opportunity to affect students even after they have discovered the opposite sex, autonomy, and roving peer groups.

At the University of North Carolina at Chapel Hill, researchers founded the Abecedarian project, a carefully controlled study that randomly selected 57 low-SES infants to receive early intervention in a high-quality child care setting up to age 5. The study assigned 54 infants with comparable life circumstances to an untreated control group. The experimental group was given developmentally appropriate activities, games, and social-emotional support. The study collected cognitive test scores from the subjects between the ages of 3 and 21 and analyzed academic test scores between the ages of 8 and 21. Sixteen years after the end of the intervention—when the subjects were 21—the treated students, on average, attained higher scores on both cognitive and academic tests (Ramey & Campbell, 1991). Compared with those in the untreated control group, youths receiving the experimental enriched treatment

- Earned higher cognitive test scores through age 21.
- Demonstrated enhanced language skills.
- Earned consistently higher reading achievement scores.
- Demonstrated moderate effect sizes in mathematics achievement.
- Were more likely to still be in school at age 21 (40 percent versus 20 percent).
- Were more likely to attend a four-year college (35 percent versus 14 percent).
- Were less likely to have experienced trouble with the legal system. (Ramey & Campbell, 1991)

Some critics charge that the IQ gains seen in the experimental group initially rose and then leveled off during late elementary and middle school. This is true; there are limits to what enrichment interventions can achieve. Yet in the area of life-skill intelligences, the Abecedarian students did very well (see Figure 3.4).

Head Start, a program born from a social-political awareness that many children living in poverty were unable to make gains from existing preschool opportunities, provides another illustration of how educational interventions can uncover human potential. This federally funded program provides economically deprived preschoolers with educational, nutritional, medical, and social services at special centers based in schools and community settings throughout the United States. Many have criticized the program for not delivering dramatic enough outcomes. But the program has been well researched, and longitudinal studies on the effectiveness of Head Start indicate that participating students demonstrate higher educational outcomes and lower occurrences of criminal activity in later years (Love et al., 2005;

3.4 Academic Benefits of Abecedarian

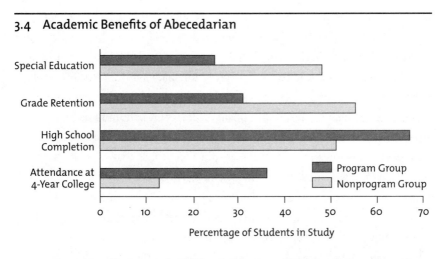

Source: Adapted from "Poverty, Early Childhood Education, and Academic Competence: The Abecedarian Experiment," by C. T. Ramey and F. A. Campbell, 1991, in A. C. Huston (Ed.), *Children in Poverty: Child Development and Public Policy* (pp. 190–221), Cambridge, UK: Cambridge University Press.

Oden, Schweinhart, & Weikart, 2000). Another study followed Head Start children into adulthood and found that some positive results continued (Schweinhart, Barnes, & Weikart, 1993).

In 2004, 900,000 children were enrolled in Head Start programs. The challenge of managing a program of this scope is difficult to fathom. The wide range of potential stumbling blocks (e.g., transience, dropout rates, and child abuse or neglect) makes it difficult to control, and some believe that Head Start's preventive intervention activities start too late for at-risk children. In 2002, soon after the first wave of local Early Head Start programs were funded, a multisite national randomized controlled trial (RCT) examined 17 of the initial 64 sites to determine whether Early Head Start programs could be successful and, if so, how they worked. Although the specific interventions varied from program to program, all of them aimed to enhance child development through relationship activities with more than one staff member, to increase parent participation, and to educate parents on child development. In addition, all the programs provided services to families and links to potentially helpful community relationships. Some programs emphasized home visits, whereas others were center-based; still others included elements of both approaches.

Results of the RCT (Love et al., 2002), which involved some 3,000 families, found that Early Head Start programs had significant positive influences on the cognitive, linguistic, and socioemotional development of 2- and 3-year-olds. The study also found positive effects on parenting based on observations of parent-child interactions and on parental self-reports. The programs that showed the strongest results were those that were independently evaluated as more fully implementing standards for quality of intervention services and continuous improvement and those that incorporated home visits as well as center components. The children in this study are now 5 and being evaluated before their entry into kindergarten. A longitudinal study is necessary to assess the extent to which the program succeeds in its goals of increasing children's readiness to learn and their socioemotional readiness for school.

The Perry Preschool in Ypsilanti, Michigan, ran a study that examined the lives of 123 African Americans born into poverty and at high risk for school failure. From 1962 to 1967, the 3- and 4-year-old subjects were randomly divided into an experimental group that received a high-quality preschool program and a control group that received no preschool program. Researchers followed up on the subjects as adults, examining their school, social services, and arrest records, and found that those who had received the preschool program earned more money, were more likely to hold a job, had committed fewer crimes, and were more likely to have graduated from high school than adults who did not attend the enrichment preschool (Weikart, 1998). Rather than providing a quick fix, the program had a ripple effect, positively influencing children's lives over the long haul. Despite the lack of clear-cut, uniform results, it is clear that early care programs *do* make a difference (Barnett, 1998), and they are worth supporting.

Action Steps

Change staff members' mind-sets. Most teachers understand that good teaching can change students. Yet some may think that IQ is fixed and that slower learners will stay slow. Encourage teachers to "brag" about students who beat the odds. Put up posters in the staff lounge stating such affirmations as "Miracles happen here every day!" and "Kids can change, and we can make it happen." Providing good staff development—even holding monthly book club meetings or distributing research articles—is essential. Begin spreading the message right away.

Invest in staff. Many schools and districts tout such slogans as "We make our students the #1 priority!" The problem is that to truly make that happen, you need staff members who feel included, supported, challenged, and nurtured—in other words, who feel that *they* are #1 as well! When you take care of your staff members, they can take care of the students. First, administer broad-based assessments to identify any gaps and ask some key questions: Does every student have a caring adult to whom he or she can go? Does every student have some connections to peers (e.g., through a buddy program or a club)? Is every student receiving an enriching curriculum that incorporates the arts and physical activity? Is every student up to par in such essential cognitive skills as vocabulary building and reading fluency? Then introduce a themed topic for the school year (e.g., targeted skill building). Provide training that addresses the chosen theme while promoting team building among staff members. Once the school year has started, implement monthly micro-training sessions to maintain momentum and accountability. The better your staff is, the better the academic achievement at your school will be.

Support ongoing collaboration. Be sure to foster strong staff relationships and team building every single school year. Staff members should know all their colleagues' names, as well as a few personal details about each one. Show staff how to make positive changes in instruction, discipline, and class environment. Educate staff about the capacity of the brain to change, and form a study group to discuss literature that examines how students change. Apply for grants, if necessary, to afford year-round staff development.

Encourage staff dialogue. Structure conversations among staff members. In the staff lounge, share success stories more than you share frustrations. If needed, have one-on-one conversations with staff members who are not yet on board. The Susan Scott book *Fierce Conversations* suggests strategies for how to start and continue difficult conversations and helps participants find a common ground and move their thinking and actions forward.

Gather quality data. Assume that you need more useful data than you already have. Test students for processing and sequencing deficits as well as memory and attention skills. Quality assessment is crucial, and follow-through even more so. Pinpointed assessments enable us to determine areas of strength and weakness. In Chapter 4, I discuss this process in more depth.

The Enrichment Mind-Set

Although the jury may still be out on the optimal type of enrichment mind-set for those working with kids in poverty, we do know for certain that the following extremes will not work:

- Focusing only on the basics (drill and kill).
- Maintaining order through a show of force.
- Eliminating or reducing time for arts, sports, and physical education.
- Increasing and intensifying classroom discipline.
- Decreasing interaction among students.
- Installing metal detectors.
- Delivering more heavy-handed top-down lectures.

Nor does it work to pity kids raised in poverty and assume that their background dooms them to failure. The first approach is simplistic and narrow-minded, and the second approach is elitist, defeatist, and, quite often, classist or racist. What works is to acknowledge that the human brain is designed to change from experiences and that if we design enough high-quality experiences, over time we will get positive change.

Although enrichment obviously has its strong points, there are some important caveats to keep in mind. Not all programs deliver on their promises. We don't often know how much enrichment is needed, and for how long, to get the maximum effect. However, the research does suggest that the worse off kids are, the greater the potential gain. If students come from good home environments, not much more than good teaching is necessary. But if students come from disadvantaged backgrounds, enrichment can have a dramatic impact on learning. And in these cases, an enrichment mind-set is crucial: every staff member must be on board and fully believe that every kid can succeed.

You'll know when everyone at your school is on board. You'll see it in the hallways, hear it in the classrooms, and feel it from the kids. You'll notice that students enjoy their classes and overall school experience and are hopeful about their future; that teachers share information and strategies with colleagues and discuss issues constructively; that the staff lounge airs more success stories than complaints; and that teachers give affirmations and support to kids all day.

The first prerequisite for change is your belief in it—and your willingness to change yourself first. At school, embody the change you want to see in students. We can help kids rise above their predicted path of struggle if we see them as possibilities, not as problems. We must stop using low IQ as an excuse for giving up on children and instead provide positive, enriching experiences that build their academic operating systems. Students' brains don't change from more of the same. We must believe that change is possible; understand that the brain is malleable and will adapt to environmental input; and be willing to change that input, too. In Chapter 4, I outline a useful model to help you in your quest.

4

Schoolwide Success Factors

Mr. Hawkins has slowly gained some exposure to a new paradigm. For years, he has been frustrated by what he has considered unacceptably poor behavior and academic performance from his low-SES students. But now he has learned that poverty creates across-the-board negative effects and produces many changes in the brain that contribute to suboptimal classroom performance. He has also learned that cognitive capacity, even IQ, is not fixed but can be improved. This new understanding has given him hope, but the buy-in process has only just begun. Although he's theoretically open to change, he's not so sure about his own school's capacity for it. Mr. Hawkins sees plenty of problems all around him. At least, he now says, "There might be something I can do before retirement. That's only six years from now."

Five SHARE Factors for Schools

By now we have seen the damage that poverty does to children's physical, social, and emotional well-being and how it leads to changes in the brain that contribute to suboptimal school behavior and performance. We have also learned that cognitive capacity is not fixed but improvable. Now it's time to do something about it.

This chapter and the next address the question, "Which policies have the greatest positive impact on the brains of students raised in poverty?" The data are abundant yet confusing; it seems that nearly every conceivable strategy has been tried. To make the task less daunting, I summarize what many researchers have published about what works and describe what I have personally seen work in schools teaching low-SES populations. The resulting model is not the *only* way a school can succeed—but it is representative of the schools that *are* succeeding.

Although low-SES and minority students typically perform more poorly than their well-off, nonminority peers do on tests of academic achievement (Reeves, 2003), some schools with high poverty and minority rates have turned these statistics around, demonstrating scores comparable with or higher than those of other schools in their districts or states. Aggregating the research from several quality studies will give us a broad base for action. Here are the studies I consulted for this purpose:

- *High Performance in High Poverty Schools: 90/90/90 and Beyond* (Reeves, 2003)
- *Inside the Black Box of High-Performing High-Poverty Schools* (Kannapel & Clements, with Taylor & Hibpshman, 2005)
- *Learning from Nine High Poverty, High Achieving Blue Ribbon Schools* (U.S. Department of Education, 2006)
- *McREL Insights: Schools That "Beat the Odds"* (Mid-continent Research for Education and Learning, 2005)
- *No Excuses: 21 Lessons from High-Performing, High-Poverty Schools* (Carter, 2000)
- *The Results Fieldbook: Practical Strategies from Dramatically Improved Schools* (Schmoker, 2001)
- *Similar Students, Different Results: Why Do Some Schools Do Better? A Large-Scale Survey of California Elementary Schools Serving Low-Income Students* (Williams et al., 2005)

In the United States, the requirement to be considered a Title I or high-poverty school is that 50 percent or more of students are eligible for free or reduced-price lunch, but I was most interested in schools with 75–100 percent of students coming from poverty. A review of the test scores of selected schools highlighted in the studies listed above suggests that the schools were considered high-performing if at least half of students had achieved a passing (proficient) score on the state standardized test. In the current age of accountability, the increased focus on school and student success as measured by standardized test scores has provided objective statistical support for certain key factors affecting achievement. High-poverty, high-achieving schools share a number of characteristics, including

- Academic press for achievement.
- Availability of instructional resources.
- Belief that all students can succeed at high levels.
- Caring staff and faculty.
- Clear curriculum choices.
- Coherent, standards-based curriculum and instructional program.
- Collaborative decision making.
- Collaborative scoring of student work.
- Dedication to diversity and equity.
- Emphasis on reading skills.
- High expectations.
- Ongoing data collection and formative assessments.
- Orderly climate.
- Regular assessment of student progress combined with feedback and remediation.
- Regular teacher-parent communication.
- Shared mission and goals.
- Strategic assignment of staff.
- Strong focus on student achievement.
- Structure (including student goals and class management).
- Support for teacher influence (teacher aides, paraprofessionals).
- Teachers' acceptance of the role they play in student success or failure.
- Unequivocal focus on academic achievement, with a no-excuses mind-set.
- Use of assessment data to improve student achievement and instruction.

The problem with this list is that although all these factors are important, no school has the time, money, or human capital to substantively change 20-plus factors at a time. So how can we translate these findings into a workable action plan? The first step is to pare the list down to a manageable focus without compromising the potency of the research invested. Accordingly, I narrowed down the list to the few factors that matter most.

First, I combined any approaches that sounded similar—for example, "strong focus on academic achievement" and "unequivocal focus on academic achievement, with a no-excuses mind-set"—as well as any approaches that were subsets or natural consequences of others. Next, I eliminated any approaches that were not "make-or-break" factors. Then I carefully scrutinized the factors that would be typically considered valuable for students from all socioeconomic backgrounds; many schools already do those well. Finally, I gave priority to any factor known to accelerate changes in the brain.

Although successful schools tend to use an integrated approach, for the purpose of clarity and simplicity I divided the approaches into two sets: schoolwide and classroom-focused. This chapter is about what it takes to make a difference at the school level; I address classroom-level approaches in Chapter 5. In each chapter, I address a set of five factors whose first initials spell out the word *SHARE* and explore each factor within the context of highly successful schools. The school-level set of factors consists of

- Support of the Whole Child.
- Hard Data.
- Accountability.
- Relationship Building.
- Enrichment Mind-Set.

Support of the Whole Child

School leaders who adopt the mantra of high expectations often demand that their students sit quietly, remain attentive, show motivation, stay out of trouble, work hard, and act polite when those students are in fact hungry, unhealthy, stressed, and emotionally stretched to the edge. The high *expectations* policy makes sense only if your students are buttressed by high *support*. Kids raised in poverty—those kids who have the greatest social, academic, emotional, and health needs—are often those who have the least access to essential human services and classroom accommodations.

Some administrators may find it inconvenient or even crazy to be expected to provide a wide-ranging net of services that other schools don't have to provide. But consider the alternatives. Most schools teaching kids from poverty do underperform, and those accountable often make excuses about "those kids." But kids who get wraparound support are able to stop dwelling on their problems and limitations and to start focusing on the educational opportunities available to them. Until your school finds ways to address the social, emotional, and health-related challenges that your kids face every day, academic excellence is just a politically correct but highly unlikely goal.

Theory and Research

To understand why these services are needed, we must go back more than half a century to Abraham Maslow's (1943) hierarchy of needs, which asserts that students cannot be expected to function at a high academic level when their basic needs—for food, shelter, medical care, safety, family, and friendships, for example—are unmet. There's an old saying that goes, "When you're up to your neck in alligators, it's hard to remember that your initial objective was to drain the swamp." For kids who are up to their necks in alligators, the secret is to provide the services that reduce their distractions and stressors and strengthen their ability to learn and succeed.

Schools that successfully educate low-SES students commonly incorporate a 360-degree wraparound student support system. Many administrators build political alliances and work to gain school board and district support in every way they can to enable them to move quickly and decisively. Without support from a wide range of agencies, the job is much tougher.

The ways schools do this are varied; some schools focus on one or two much-needed areas of support, whereas others try to cover almost everything. In addition to the standard range of support services, some students may need additional accommodations to succeed. Kids raised in poverty are more likely to have disabilities than middle- and upper-income kids are. As a result, educators should be extra vigilant in discovering ways to support their least advantaged learners. All students with active Individualized Education Plans (IEPs) or 504 Plans are entitled to the appropriate accommodations to empower them to fully participate in state- and districtwide testing. Legally, accommodations must be specified in the IEP, but this requirement does not prohibit teachers from using good judgment with resource allocation or from making the occasional sensible exception to the rule. Accommodations as simple as providing a quiet place for a student to take a test can lessen the effects of students' disabilities or disadvantages.

High-Poverty Schools Making It Happen

The Preuss School in La Jolla, California, is a public charter school with 760 middle and high school students, 94 percent of whom are minorities and 100 percent of whom are eligible for free or reduced-price lunch. Yet the school's graduation rates are through the roof, and more than 95 percent of its graduates are accepted to and attend four-year colleges. In their 2008 rankings, both *Newsweek* and *U.S. News & World Report* included Preuss in their lists of the top 10 high schools in the United States.

What does The Preuss School do differently? In short, it refuses to let students fail. As with many successful schools, the staff has high expectations. But the school buttresses those expectations with 360-degree student support. The school year is a nonstop enrichment program. Specifically, Preuss offers

- A health care department partnership with the University of California, San Diego, supported by a foundation grant that allows access to medical care on a referral basis and provides a physician to work with teachers, a nurse practitioner for adolescent health, and an on-site nurse.
- Full-time resource specialists for students with Individualized Education Plans and roving resource specialists for students with speech, hearing, or physical disabilities.
- A district psychologist, available for testing and counseling, and a private psychologist, available to students for on-site, no-cost therapy.
- Teachers who regularly participate in problem-solving sessions with students and families to help improve coping capacity.
- Tutoring in every subject by qualified university tutors who take the time to ensure that students will succeed at their work.
- On-campus internships for students.

At Preuss, no student feels alone, ignored, or burdensome. Kids' parents know that anything they are unable to provide for their kids' academic success is likely to be provided at school. The feeling of support that kids get at Preuss may be what contributes to their high attendance and graduation rates. This wraparound support fosters stronger, more disciplined student effort. Although it may be surprising to hear it, self-discipline actually counts more than IQ when it comes to academic achievement (see Figure 4.1).

4.1 Self-Discipline Beats IQ

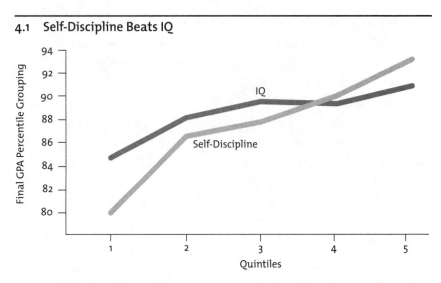

A two-year study of 8th graders revealed that self-discipline was a significantly better predictor of academic performance than IQ. This graph depicts final grade point average as a function of ranked quintiles of IQ and self-discipline.

Source: Adapted from "Self-Discipline Outdoes IQ in Predicting Academic Performance of Adolescents," by A. L. Duckworth and M. P. Seligman, 2005, *Psychological Science, 16*(12), pp. 939–944.

Action Steps

Survey your student needs. When kids are preoccupied with essential safety, health, and relational issues, they cannot focus on academics. Consult your school's counselors and special education teachers about the accommodations that make sense for students. The most common support services students need include

- Academic and alternative tutoring.
- Academic, career, or mental health counseling.
- Access to medications.
- Child care for teen parents.
- Community services (housing and utilities).
- Dental care.
- Life skills classes in finances, health, housing, and so on.
- Medical care, both urgent and long-term.

- Psychology (diagnosis and therapy).
- Reading materials.
- Transportation for when students stay late for after-school help.

Include parents and provide adult support and outreach. Build strong, long-term relationships, identify the most critical areas of need, and offer content that parents need most. Offer on-site programs on such topics as nutrition, parenting, and study skill coaching for children.

Develop community partnerships. Schools obviously have limited funding, yet many community agencies have the resources and the will to donate or partner with you to provide needed support services. You might arrange

- Free medical services (donated by a local hospital).
- Free tutoring (provided by nearby university students who get academic or volunteer credits).
- Free mental health services (by retired psychologists or therapists).
- Free books (donated by the library, clubs, the Rotary Club, parents, and so on).

Each child has a limited set of internal resources for dealing with everyday worries as well as bigger stressors. Once that capacity is maxed out, the first casualty is school. Why? When kids are worried about being evicted or living in abusive households, doing well in school barely makes it onto the to-do list. If you have a painful, persistent toothache, the teacher's well-designed lesson seems irrelevant. To get kids to focus on academic excellence, we must remove the real-world concerns that are much higher on their mental and emotional priority lists.

Hard Data

A key feature of high-performing schools is an unwillingness to accept state or district tests as the sole measures of achievement. Successful schools generate their own high-quality, useful data on an ongoing basis and provide immediate feedback to both students and teachers.

Every student is an individual with his or her own learning styles, needs, and skills; teachers can't be expected to intuit these for each student. That's why schools need to collect accurate, relevant, and specific data in a timely fashion. With high-quality data on student performance, teachers can continually adjust their instructional decisions, and students can modify their learning strategies.

The three most important steps to becoming a data-friendly school are (1) selling teachers on the value of data so that they can teach smarter, not harder; (2) creating a culture of continual data collection, analysis, and application; and (3) emphasizing that using data to improve the teaching process is a sign of professionalism, not an acquiescence to failure. Data tell us that students' IQ scores do not determine their destiny. Everyone at your school should know that a staggering number of kids perform much better than their IQ scores predict they will. What matter more to their success potential are their emotional skill sets and the sheer effort they put in (see Figure 4.2).

Theory and Research

Specific, ongoing data collection is a must for success in all schools, but especially in high-poverty ones. Multiple studies suggest that data can

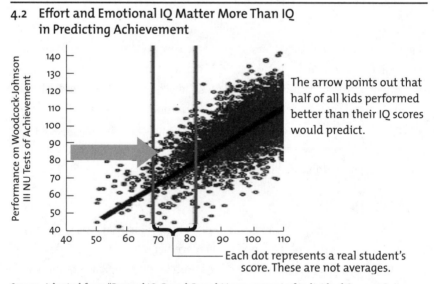

4.2 Effort and Emotional IQ Matter More Than IQ in Predicting Achievement

The arrow points out that half of all kids performed better than their IQ scores would predict.

Each dot represents a real student's score. These are not averages.

Source: Adapted from "Beyond IQ: Broad-Based Measurement of Individual Success Potential or 'Emotional Intelligence,'" by A. Mehrabian, 2002, *Genetic, Social, & General Psychology Monographs, 126*(2), pp. 133–239.

support school inquiry and drive achievement gains (Herman & Gribbons, 2001). The factors that most determine data's effectiveness are the quality, accuracy, and timeliness of the data; the school's capacity for data disaggregation; the collaborative use of data organized around a clear set of questions; and leadership structures that support schoolwide use of data (Lachat & Smith, 2005). Successful schools effectively analyze the information and then adjust school policies and instructional strategies accordingly (Williams et al., 2005).

This cycle of continual assessment and adjustment, known as formative assessment, must be ongoing, purposeful, and customized for your school. Formative assessments show you exactly where your students stand at any given time. If your data point to gaps in the school climate, you can work on that. If your data show gaps in student learning, focus on building skills to upgrade students' academic operating systems. Evidence (National Education Association, 2003) suggests that when given clear, current, and useful data, most teachers are willing to make changes. Assessment expert W. James Popham (2008) suggests that formative assessment improves teaching, learning, classroom climate, professional development of teachers, and school performance. Formative assessment can turn the classroom into a collaboration between students and teachers to reach agreed-upon learning goals.

High-Poverty Schools Making It Happen

At Sampit Elementary School, located in rural South Carolina, 90 percent of students receive free or reduced-price lunch. In 2000, Sampit's test scores were considered below average. Since that time, Sampit has become a high-achieving school, with more than 85 percent of its students having achieved at least a Basic rating in English language arts and math. Educators at Sampit study prior or pre-assessment data and ongoing assessment data from state and district assessments at meetings designed for this purpose. At these meetings, participants set goals for improvement, identify students needing additional interventions, and plan these interventions. At subsequent meetings, they review the new data to determine whether goals have been met using specific, continuous, accurate, relevant, and timely collection, interpretation, and application of data.

At Ira Harbison Elementary in National City, California, instruction is driven by formative assessment data, and students are divided into small groups according to their needs. Teachers receive training in the data management programs, which help them organize the data in meaningful ways and determine instructional groupings. Ira Harbison not only provides students with computer-driven instruction but also provides teachers with ongoing, pertinent reports of student strengths and weaknesses, both for individual students and for whole classes.

Watson Williams, a secondary magnet school for the performing arts in Utica, New York, uses computer-assisted instruction and frequent assessments to yield data that drive instruction on a daily basis. Teachers meet before school for 15 minutes each day (with grade-level colleagues Monday through Thursday and with subject-level colleagues Friday) to review assessment data and make instructional decisions based on them. The school also conducts detailed item analyses from state test results and investigates items on which students score below the district average. Through this process, the school has identified deficits in such areas as vocabulary and integrated the content into the curriculum at every grade level.

Action Steps

Good teaching is not magic, and it is not based solely on intuition. To guide you in tailoring the strengths of your staff and faculty to the individual instructional needs of your students, you need a rigorous program of data analysis and application. When your teachers create and embrace a culture of continuous data collection and use, they will teach smarter. Turnaround schools typically create reports at regular intervals on a variety of indicators, set up internal databases to capture data normally sent to the district or to generate data at a finer grain size than required by the district, and hold regular meetings to act on any concerns generated by the data.

Develop criteria for the data you need. If you go to your doctor with a knee problem, the doctor will check your symptoms, look at your medical history, conduct mobility testing, and possibly order an MRI. Similarly, your school must collect multiple forms of data for each student. Asking questions about the school's current performance is a good place to start. Gather data that answer three core questions:

1. **Both generally and specifically, how are we doing?** You can break
this down to grade level, subject area, and micro skills (e.g., How are we
doing with text comprehension levels for 4th grade boys?)

2. **To what degree are we serving the needs of all students?** You must
be brutally honest in asking this and related questions (e.g., How many
tardies, suspensions, or referrals have we had in the last month? Who is
getting them, and who is giving them?).

3. **What are we good at, and where do we need help?** Your school
might be good in some areas (e.g., staff morale) but weak in others (e.g.,
teaching key learning-to-learn skills).

Have staff members respond to these questions anonymously using simple
half-sheets of paper. Tally the results, present them at a staff meeting, and
use the answers as a springboard for the change process. For the purposes
of this survey, give equal weight to standardized assessment results and findings from school-based assessments targeting the cultural, academic, and
social issues most relevant to your own school. Answering these questions
can stimulate additional detailed questions about the what and the how of
student performance. Ron Fitzgerald, a former superintendent of a high-
performing high school, is now a consultant who has established his own list
of questions to determine which data to collect and how to analyze them:

1. What is each student's status on the knowledge, skills, and attitudes to
be covered in a course, class, or unit?

2. What are each student's learning styles, strengths, weaknesses, and
special interests?

3. Does the student need additional assistance during or after a specific
learning segment?

4. What final learning can you celebrate and document for each student?

5. Based on learning outcomes and discussion with students, what
changes can you make to improve the effectiveness of your teaching in
the future?

Gather only the data you need. It may take some time for your school
to reach this point. Most schools initially under- or overcollect data. You'll
need to answer questions about every aspect of students' present state

of performance, but too much data can overwhelm a staff. Keep yourself sane by setting a limited number of measurable achievement goals for the lowest-scoring students and targeting the specific standards where achievement is lowest.

Use multiple data sources (e.g., interim classroom test results, student portfolios, teacher-created strength analyses, or schoolwide student inventories) to answer your questions and different data sets to provide different kinds of information about student performance. Resist the common temptation to use a single form of data to understand your students; it won't be enough. To be useful, data sets must focus on the academic issues that matter most, including working memory (Automated Working Memory Assessment [AWMA], Working Memory Rating Scale [WMRS], or Working Memory Test Battery [WMTB-C]); language (Speed and Capacity of Language Processing Test [SCOLP]); and sequencing and processing (Woodcock-Johnson III). These skills enhance students' abilities to meet academic requirements, and all of them can be honed.

The better your school gets at data gathering, the more specific your data requirements will become. But first and foremost, your data must be *specific, continuous, accurate, relevant,* and *fast.* SCARF is a handy mnemonic to keep these essential qualities in mind.

Keep tweaking the quantity of data. You'll be able to mine existing data by collecting and managing relevant information on school performance and characteristics. But you'll also need the relatively new data forms mentioned above.

Analyze and share the data. You will need to be able to translate data for educators, parents, community members, and policymakers, so your data should be user-friendly. You may have some in-house resources to do this for you, but if not, you may be able to get help from a nearby university or psychologist or a data analysis firm. Although the task of comprehensive data collection and analysis may seem daunting, there are many simple and easy-to-understand visual tools available, including

- Spreadsheet databases.
- Column charts that allow visual comparison.
- Pareto charts to identify priorities.

- Run charts or line charts to display trends.
- Scatter charts to show relationships or correlations.
- Rubrics to measure performance against standards or to analyze strengths and weaknesses in individual or group performance.
- Cause-and-effect diagrams.
- Story-boarding panels.

The data must be in a coherent and actionable form. Do not overwhelm your staff with endless eye-glazing tables of information. One of the best ways to present the data is in clear visual formats. To get some ideas on how to make your data more user-friendly, go to www.visual-literacy.org/pages/documents.htm and click on "Periodic Table" for a useful example of a fresh, effective presentation tool (Lengler & Eppler, 2007).

Develop plans to apply the data. Top schools avoid "paralysis by analysis." Here is a recommended scenario:

1. Consult assessment data to identify your school's areas of lowest performance, and then set a limited number of goals addressing those deficits.
2. Work with staff to find better ways to teach the necessary skills and continuously refine these strategies by using a baseline and measuring the number of students who actually learn the targeted skills.
3. Create a specific plan and put it into action.

Here's an example of this process in practice. At one school, only 4 percent of students reached the writing standard in "descriptive settings." The teacher team checked the interpretive guide to the state assessment to learn what an effective descriptive setting looked like. In less than 30 minutes, they sketched out an effective lesson for addressing this deficit. They implemented the lesson and assessed progress weekly. In a short time, the teachers got an astonishing 94 percent of students to write high-quality descriptive settings. One half-hour meeting and one month of implementation of the lesson plan achieved clear results (Schmoker, 2002).

It's not hard to foster a more data-friendly culture in your school. You can begin by encouraging your teachers to share information about students with one another, discussing who needs help and what has worked with individual students in the past. Have them set three to five measurable achievement goals in the lowest-scoring subjects or courses and work together to design, modify, and assess instructional strategies that directly target low student performance on specific standards.

Accountability

Talk to kids in unsuccessful schools, and they might tell you about school facilities that are falling apart, or about teachers who don't know the subjects they are teaching, or who lecture without bothering to engage their students, or who dismiss their students' life problems as trivial. Ask teachers in unsuccessful schools why low-SES kids usually don't succeed, and they will often blame students' poverty, decry the violence in the neighborhood, explain away students' lack of motivation, or point fingers at parents' neglect. Their reasons, in other words, amount to stories and excuses. To these teachers, it's all about the problems inherent in disadvantaged children's circumstances. Ultimately, all we educators have are our stories or our results. Those who don't get results often cling to their stories about why success eludes them. Those who get results simply point to the numbers and say, "We did it!"

You cannot assign a sense of responsibility to teachers. Responsibility is a moral and ethical sensitivity to the effects of our actions. A relevant, emotional before-and-after story from a turnaround student may effectively demonstrate to teachers how much their actions matter; then again, it may not. Responsibility is a character quality that staff members have to choose for themselves. Accountability, on the other hand, is part of the job description. Every teacher is accountable for his or her actions and can be evaluated with quality data. The best way to achieve accountability is to create a compelling, collaborative goal and then to administer formative assessments that provide useful, specific data demonstrating progress toward that goal.

Ultimately, teachers will have to buy into the process, commit to teaching "smarter," and learn to adjust their practice on the fly to reach collective goals. If your teachers stay the course and follow through, your school will probably achieve some measure of success. Figure 4.3 demonstrates what a difference high levels of dedication and implementation make.

4.3 Gains in Standard Deviation at Three Levels of Implementation of SHARE Factors

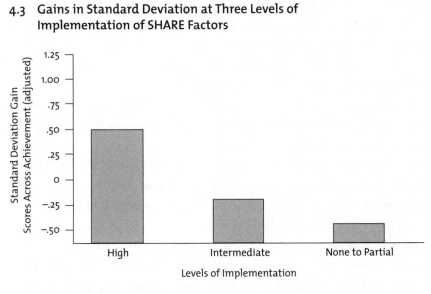

Levels of Implementation

Source: Adapted from "Examining the Role of Implementation Quality in School-Based Prevention Using the PATHS Curriculum," by C. Kam, M. Greenberg, and C. Walls, 2003, *Prevention Science, 4*(1).

Theory and Research

A key premise of this book is that brains are designed to change, adapting from life experiences for better or worse. The degree of change you can elicit in your students is directly proportional to these factors:

1. **Positive contrast.** How do the conditions you create contrast with your students' prevailing everyday experiences? If your school days are "more of the same," you can expect to see few positive effects. Enrichment programs are beneficial only if they clearly improve on the home environment in ways that directly affect measured outcomes (Barnett, 1995).

2. **Consistent sustainability.** For many low-SES children, a Montessori preschool can work wonders all the way through middle school, because it offers a more enriched curriculum than many low-performing schools do (Miller & Bizzell, 1984). But your school doesn't need to be a private school to succeed; it needs to provide consistent enrichment over time.

Let's assume you're implementing the *SHARE* factors in this chapter. Will implementation alone guarantee success? Passion comes from feeling responsible and accountable for results, which means it's the rigor, intensity, and duration of the enriching education you provide that matters. Let's do the math. Here's what your staff is up against:

1. Every student in your school gets 168 hours each week (7 days × 24 hours).
2. Subtract the time kids spend on sleeping, eating, grooming, dealing with medical and transportation issues, looking after siblings, moving, and dealing with family emergencies and a host of other disruptions (12–13 hours per day × 7 days = 84–91 hours).
3. That leaves each child with a *maximum* of 84 hours each week, or 4,368 hours each year. Out of that block, you get, at most, 30 school hours each week (6 hours × 5 days) for 36 to 42 weeks per year. At the high end, you get 1,260 hours each year (30 hours per week × 42 weeks) for changing student lives.
4. Here's the key ratio: 1,260 hours out of a possible 4,368. You have 28 percent of a student's waking time. You are outnumbered by more than two to one.

The significance of that number—28 percent—is profound. There is very little you can do about students' home lives, or about the people with whom they associate. With the small proportion of their lives that you *do* have access to, you cannot afford to waste a single class or school day. You cannot afford to put a student down or treat him unfairly. You cannot afford to bore a student or fail to engage her in class. You cannot suspend a student for anything frivolous; in fact, the more days students spend out of school, the less chance you have of success. School needs to be a nonstop bobsled run, full of activity, challenge, correction, support, and enrichment. You need to challenge students to do their best every hour of every day they are in your charge. Unless your school is doing this month after month, year after year, you have no chance. If you surrender to the despair and deprivation of students' lives outside school, you will make your classroom and school failure a self-fulfilling prophecy. To get the best from your students, you must expect and demand the best from yourself.

If you are serious about helping students from poverty to succeed, keep this in mind: your 1,260 hours have to be so spectacular that they can overcome the other 7,500 hours in your students' lives. Is your school that good?

High-Poverty Schools Making It Happen

Every time you read the success story of a turnaround school, you'll find that it has high expectations that are embraced—not just parroted—by the entire staff. The El Paso, Texas, community has taken the no-excuses, high-expectations mind-set to heart. Despite their city's extraordinarily high poverty rate, local education leaders set some very high accountability standards for what their students should know and be able to do. And unlike other communities, they didn't stop there. Faculty members at the University of Texas, El Paso, felt accountable, too. So they revamped the way the university prepared teachers. Since the university implemented these changes, preservice elementary teachers, for example, take more than twice as much math and science as their predecessors did. The teachers of these courses are math and science professors who themselves participated in the standard-setting process and who know at a deep level what kinds of mathematical understanding the teachers need.

The community also formed a group known as the El Paso Collaborative to provide support to existing teachers and to help them teach to the new standards. The collaborative sponsored intensive summer workshops, monthly meetings for teachers within content areas, and work sessions in schools to analyze student assignments against the standards. The three school districts within El Paso also released 60 teachers to coach their peers. The results are clear: no more low-performing schools, and increased expectations and achievement for *all groups of students,* with even bigger increases among the groups that have historically been left behind (Ferguson & Meyer, 2001). El Paso and similarly successful communities have a lot to teach us about how to raise overall achievement and close gaps.

At Lapwai Elementary School in Idaho, the student population is mostly made up of low-SES American Indian children, of whom 95 percent are reading at or above grade level. The secret? Everyone at the school has accepted his or her share of responsibility and feels accountable for the results. The teachers assign tough work and expect the students to do it—and do it right. What matters is a relentless focus on the academic core, on clear and high standards, and on accountability systems that demand results for all kinds of students—all supported by intensive efforts to help teachers improve their practice and to provide extra instruction for students who need it. Instead of making excuses, the school lays down the gauntlet of excellence and provides teachers who know and care about the subjects they are teaching and spend every moment of class engaging students (Parrett, 2005).

You see this same pathway in the 65-plus KIPP (Knowledge Is Power Program) schools that teach more than 16,000 students in 20 U.S. states. KIPP school populations are more than 90 percent African American and Latino, and more than 80 percent of KIPP students are eligible for free or reduced-price meals. Students are accepted regardless of their prior academic records, conduct, or socioeconomic backgrounds. Yet KIPP students consistently qualify for acceptance to universities. How? High standards, enrichment, and the support to make it happen. In addition, KIPP provides teachers with more hours to work with kids by extending the school day and the school year, which begins in July. Students attend school from 7:30 a.m. to 5:00 p.m. Monday through Thursday (on Fridays, they are released at 2:30 p.m.) and on alternating Saturdays. The accountability at the KIPP schools is strong, and it shows.

Action Steps

Increase teachers' control and authority. In general, teachers are more willing to become accountable when they have some say-so over the processes involved. Give teachers input in such matters as

- Team teaching.
- Facility management.
- Staff development.
- Curriculum and use of materials.
- Budgeting decisions.
- Personnel changes.

- Schoolwide decision making.
- Shared school management.
- Administrative processes.

Value your teachers. Many teachers feel underpaid, undervalued, and overworked. Quit assuming that staff members are tireless workhorse volunteers and understand that they have many "gears" they work at and emotional levels they bring to the job each day. You can also

- Share research findings demonstrating that each year students have good teachers, their test scores improve.
- Make sure you acknowledge staff at formal meetings, in the classroom, and in the hallway.
- Hold fun "awards assembly" parties at which every staff member does something nice for a selected colleague.
- Celebrate your teachers: ensure that administrative staff notices when a teacher does something out of the ordinary, or call a local paper to do a story on a standout teacher.
- Stop wasting staff time by delivering administrative information in meetings that might better be handled by e-mail.

Redesign staffing roles. An old adage states that once the classroom door is closed, teaching is a lonely job. It doesn't have to be that way. Class schedules can be revamped to allow for extended team teaching. Teachers can share blocks of students (e.g., 4 teachers can look after 120 students and continually change the ratios and teaming), classrooms, and resource rooms. Create a "flattened" school bureaucracy to make administrators' role more supportive and less supervisory. In addition,

- Provide teacher support services (e.g., health services, time to run errands, time off).
- Reassign support staff (e.g., create shared services and new roles).
- Provide common planning time (e.g., early or late planning or midday rotating segments with partial staff while other staff doubles up assignments).
- Fund the process of joint planning to ensure enough time and money for all.
- Share classrooms and labs to reduce costs and increase collegiality.

We know that students have the ability to learn even the most challenging work, regardless of race or socioeconomic status. Schools that hold themselves accountable for students' success do not give low-SES and minority students remedial coursework or keep them from rigorous classes because of their economic backgrounds and home lives. Teachers are typically hesitant to become more accountable unless they have the resources to succeed. If your staff does not feel accountable, there may be good reasons for it. Even if your school has a challenging curriculum and a culture of high expectations, change will not happen unless you support and nurture your teachers. For many teachers, change is hard. Some teachers are unwilling to change, and for some it may take a year or two. Be patient, and do not quit on a teacher until you have exhausted other options.

Relationship Building

Secure attachments and stable environments, so vitally important to young children's healthy social and emotional development, are often severely lacking in low-income homes. Poverty stunts the formation of healthy relationships. Overworked, overstressed, and undereducated low-SES parents are more inclined to demonstrate a lack of interest in and neglect or negativity toward their children. Not getting the opportunity to form solid attachments initiates a stream of long-term physiological, psychological, and sociological consequences for children.

Theory and Research

Relationships come in many forms, and each exerts a different kind of force on our lives. In some cases, the forces are subtle, working their magic over time. In other cases, the forces are more like a blunt trauma. Relationships that matter at your school include

- Students' relationships with their peers.
- Caregivers' relationships with their children.
- School staff members' relationships with one another.
- Teachers' relationships with students.

As we saw in Chapter 2, low-SES children often experience impaired relational experiences. It starts early for most; impoverished parents are often dealing with the chronic stress of poverty, struggling just to stay afloat (Keegan-Eamon & Zuehl, 2001), which results in less attention, support, and affection for the developing child. Outside the home, children in poverty are more likely to describe feeling deprived, embarrassed, picked on, or bullied. These children feel isolated and unworthy in their younger years and often become depressed or even psychologically disturbed as they come of age and face struggles in marital and other relationships. Children who learn early on that they cannot rely on those closest to them and who are left to suffer repeated hurts of isolation, criticism, and disappointment find it more difficult to rise above their circumstances (Mikulincer & Shaver, 2001). The implications for classrooms are profound: no curriculum, instruction, or assessment, however high-quality, will succeed in a hostile social climate.

Children's lack of secure attachments is manifested in the classroom through bids for attention, acting out, and anxiety. Commonly, kids display an "I don't need anyone's help" attitude. This attitude keeps the child at a safe distance from a world that has provided no reliable relationships. When students exhibit these behaviors, don't take them personally. Instead, be empathetic and make yourself a source of reliable support. Early chaos in a child's life is highly disruptive, and without any stable, positive relationships, kids typically develop a host of behavioral problems. The good news is that schools can provide the resources not just to help students form new attachments but also to reverse the damage already done.

The assumption that students from poverty won't succeed at school because of their home lives is not supported by research. Teachers are in an opportune position to provide strong relationship support. According to Lee and Burkam (2003), students were less likely to drop out and more likely to graduate when they felt a positive bond with teachers and others at school. The one-on-one attention and nurturing guidance that come from lower student-teacher ratios enable children to succeed academically and help improve their self-esteem.

A study by Finn and Achilles (1999) of 1,803 low-SES minority students found that self-esteem and school engagement were among the most important factors keeping kids in school. Another study (Kretovics, Farber, & Armaline, 2004) examined the ALeRT (Accelerated Learning, culturally Responsive Teaching) centers. These projects work to improve schools' performance by developing a comprehensively supportive learning community and by providing ongoing professional development for teachers. Teachers, coaches, and counselors can do a great deal to instill in kids a more hopeful and future-oriented view of their school experience.

One of the easiest and most successful ways to build strong relationships is to implement "looping," a strategy that keeps a cohort of students with the same teachers from one grade level to the next. This practice builds a stronger family atmosphere and fosters more consistent and coherent student-teacher interaction. This "carryover" relationship is also academically beneficial: in the second year of a loop, the class doesn't have to start from scratch and can gain up to six additional weeks of instructional time. Looping helps teachers create curricular continuity from one year to the next; kids are less likely to fall through the cracks or get "passed off" to another teacher. At the elementary level, looping works well over a three-year span, but at the middle and high school levels, looping works best over two-year spans because of greater student turnover and transfer rates. Looping is correlated with

- Improved reading and math performance (Hampton, Mumford, & Bond, 1997).
- Emotional stability and improved conflict resolution and teamwork (Checkley, 1995).
- Stronger bonds and increased involvement among students, teachers, and caregivers (Checkley, 1995).
- Higher attendance rates, lower retention rates, and fewer special education referrals (Hampton et al., 1997).

Although strong student-parent relationships are ideal, students often seek out and value relationships with teachers, counselors, and mentors. Teachers who are sensitive to their students and who openly share their enthusiasm for learning and their belief in their students' abilities can help buffer low-SES kids from the many risks and stressors they experience in their lives (Zhang & Carrasquillo, 1995). Disadvantaged elementary students who felt connected with their teachers showed improvements in their reading and vocabulary abilities (Pianta & Stuhlman, 2004), and in the higher grades, minority students who had a math teacher of the same race and gender were more likely to enroll in higher-level math courses, thereby significantly improving their odds of graduating from college (Klopfenstein, 2004). And teens who have had a long-term relationship with a mentor enjoy higher self-esteem, better health, less involvement with gangs or violence, more exposure to positive social norms, and better outcomes at school and work (DuBois & Silverthorn, 2005). Mentors can model a passion for learning, offer academic help, build strong relationships, and direct students to services as needed. Jekielek, Moore, and Hair (2002) found that, compared with students in a nonmentored control group, mentored students

- Were more optimistic about their academics.
- Were less likely to miss or skip school or class.
- Engaged in fewer antisocial activities.
- Were less likely to initiate drug or alcohol use.
- Earned higher GPAs.
- Were less likely to hit someone.
- Were less likely to lie to a parent.
- Experienced better peer relationships.
- Were more likely to give emotional support to classmates and friends.

One of the key ingredients in mentoring is longevity (DuBois & Silverthorn, 2004), and this is an area where high school athletic programs have proven especially beneficial. An in-depth survey (Newman, 2005) of coaches and their impact on male students' academic performance found that most of the coaches were highly involved with their student athletes. Two-thirds of the coaches said in the survey that they took time to talk with students individually and to follow up with teachers and parents about the students' academic performance. Likewise, more than 80 percent of the student athletes said that they believed their coach cared about their grades, and three-fourths of the students rated their coach as one of the top three most influential people in their lives (Newman, 2005). Because students are more likely to stick with a sport that they start off playing, their involvement in athletic programs greatly increases the likelihood of having the long-term emotional support of a positive adult role model (Herrera et al., 2007). Not surprisingly, athletic programs have been found to increase rates of academic performance and graduation and to reduce behavioral problems in schools (Ratey & Hagerman, 2008; Sallis et al., 1999).

Up to this point, this section has addressed relationship building through socialization, which encourages your students to seek acceptance by being like others. The quest for social status exerts equal pressure on students but is just the opposite: it creates competition within a group to be better. Humans everywhere strive for high social status because the world seems to bestow more privileges on those who have it. Schools aren't immune: the highest-achieving students are named on the Dean's List, and athletic teams choose their Most Valuable Players. People will strive to get to the top rung of whatever social ladder they occupy. Kids, too, collect data through experiences and have a pretty good idea of where they rank in class, in their neighborhood, on the dance floor, or on a sports team. Now, what's the significance of this status seeking?

If a student perceives that he or she cannot reach the top tier in social status, then acceptance becomes even more important. One well-designed study (Kirkpatrick & Ellis, 2001) teased apart the distinction between status and acceptance. Students who felt they were high-status tended to be more aggressive (think of famous athletes, politicians, or gang leaders), whereas those who felt accepted were less aggressive. The assertive quest for status may put some students at odds with students who also want their group (and peer) acceptance.

What you want to emphasize at school is moderate social status and group acceptance. The best thing you and your staff can do is include, include, include. Help students feel accepted for who they are, and give them all micro-niches for status by finding some tasks or narrow skill or knowledge sets at which they excel. Poor or weak relationships generate a host of negative effects, including chronic elevated levels of cortisol, which can destroy new brain cells, impair social judgment, reduce memory, and diminish cognition (Sapolsky, 2005). But when students feel accepted, have sufficient social status, and maintain positive relationships, they bloom academically. Over the long haul, honing students' so-called "soft skills" is just as important as building their academic operating systems (Hawkins, Guo, Hill, Battin-Pearson, & Abbott, 2001; Hawkins, Kosterman, Catalano, Hill, & Abbott, 2008).

High-Poverty Schools Making It Happen

The Healthy Kids Mentoring Program, which paired at-risk 4th graders with specially trained mentors from the community, found that keeping mentoring sessions linked with the school improved students' feelings of bonding and inclusion at school (King, Vidourek, Davis, & McClellan, 2002). After one semester of mentoring, nearly three-fourths of the students—who had previously been failing two or more classes—saw improvements in their grades and reading skills (King et al., 2002). Other benefits included improved self-esteem and better relationships with family, peers, and school faculty (King et al., 2002).

Nearly three-fourths of the student body at Belle Chasse Primary School in Belle Chasse, Louisiana, is eligible for free or reduced-price meals. Yet the school's 4th graders scored third-highest in the entire state in mathematics and sixth-highest in English language arts (view the scores online at www.publicschoolreview.com/school_ov/school_id/34499). This Blue Ribbon school had the fewest number of unsatisfactory scores (4 percent) of any school in the state. It's no coincidence that the school makes relationships a priority. The former principal, Cynthia Hoyle, created a structured but family-like school climate. The principals know every single kid in the school by name. Teachers send weekly notes home to parents. School leaders support the staff, and staff members support the children. When disaster or tragedy strikes (the school was hit hard by Hurricane Katrina in 2005), the staff jumps right into "How can we help?" mode. This bonding creates an extraordinary level of responsiveness—even a healthy sense of mutual obligation. The students want to do better because the staff cares so much. They don't want to let anyone down.

Action Steps

Build relationships among staff. Your students can see whether staff members get along and support one another. A divided staff influences students' perceptions about the value of relationships, and when staff members aren't on the same page, odds of success drop dramatically. Therefore, staff collaboration and collegiality are key to making your school work. Teachers should reach agreements on vision, goals, methods, micro-targets, and even scoring rubrics. Interdisciplinary, collaborative teams can create targeted, data-driven instructional practices, including small-group instruction, matching assessment criteria, and cross-checking of student portfolios to discover strengths and weaknesses. To build stronger relationships among staff members and increase their effectiveness,

- Hold informal events such as celebrations of success, all-staff retreats, going-away parties, or holiday events.
- Plan short team-building staff development programs or activities that get colleagues discussing their backgrounds, strengths, and hobbies.
- Set up temporary councils or committees to address such issues as school safety, parent concerns, academic achievement, and district mandates.
- Encourage teachers to partner with grade-level or subject-area colleagues for lesson planning, grading, and rubric development.
- Engage staff in school improvement efforts by having them collect data, share ideas, and participate in staff development sessions.

The format of staff-to-staff interactions is less important than the degree to which school staff members feel ownership—that they have some control over the change process. Certainly, the mere existence of mechanisms to stimulate interaction does not guarantee staff involvement, but the successful reforms I studied devised a number of promising strategies, such as off-campus faculty social events, team-building activities, and grade-level or content-level work teams.

Build relationships among students. Students who know, trust, and cooperate with one another typically do better academically. Often mentioned but too rarely used, cooperative learning is a powerful strategy that enables students to play different roles (e.g., leader, recorder, speaker, and organizer) in multiple relationships with other students. Use the first week of school as a time for students to share their strengths ("I can fix any tech problem"), hobbies ("I really like collecting baseball cards"), and stories ("When I was in 2nd grade I had a crush on a cafeteria worker"). Divide the class into pairs and ask students to learn three things about their partners. Then have students introduce their partners to the rest of the class.

Students will have a hard time bonding with peers and doing well academically unless they feel safe, appreciated, important, and supported. The following survey, which you may want to distribute after the first 30 days of school, provides you with a starting point:

1. **Do you feel safe at school?** If so, what is it that helps you feel safe? If not, what would make you feel safer?
2. **Do you belong and fit in with others?** If so, what is it that helps you feel like you belong? If not, what would help make you feel like you belong?
3. **Are you in good standing with others?** If so, what is it that helps you feel important? If not, what do you think would boost your status?
4. **Are you supported?** If so, what is it that helps you feel supported? If not, what would ensure greater support?

Build student-staff relationships. This may seem obvious, but for kids raised in poverty, it's a make-or-break factor. Treat students with respect, and you'll get it back. To strengthen these relationships,

- Avoid raising your voice unless it's an emergency.
- Do what you say you are going to do.
- Acknowledge a change in plans if you need to make one.
- Always say "please" and "thank you"; never demand what you want.
- Take responsibility for any mistakes you make, and make amends.
- Be consistent and fair to all students; show no favoritism.
- Offer support in helping students reach their goals.
- Positively reinforce students when they do something right.
- Show that you care more than you show authority or knowledge.

Many schools rely on power and authority rather than positive relationships to get students to behave or perform well. The problem with the coercion approach is simple: the weaker the relationships, the more resources and authority you need to get the same job done. If a staff member needs help carrying supplies out to her car, and she has good relationships with her students, she is likely to get not one but several volunteers. People will do more, and do it more willingly, for people they respect and enjoy being around.

The Midwest Educational Reform Consortium (MERC) has suggested that a school can "act like a small school" even if it isn't one. Such schools are generally safer, more effective, more inviting, and higher-achieving. They tend to incorporate more team teaching, less ability grouping, less academic departmentalization, and smaller student groupings.

There's a huge difference between an *orderly* school, where things run smoothly, and an *ordered* school, which follows a top-down authoritarian model. The former respects students; the latter treats them like second-class citizens. For every teacher who complains about all the things that "those kids" won't do, there are plenty of teachers who rejoice that their students would do anything for them. Relationships will make or break your school. Do not fool yourself into thinking that students' feelings about themselves, their peers, and their teachers are unimportant. On the contrary, most students care more than anything about who cares about them! Adults who build trusting, supportive relationships with low-SES students help foster those students' independence and self-esteem and protect them from the deleterious effects of poverty. Principals, teachers, counselors, and coaches must provide the much-needed outstretched hand that will help children lift themselves out of the poverty cycle.

Enrichment Mind-Set

Doing the same thing over and over and expecting a different result is a recipe for failure. Your school will get results only when you and your staff shift your collective mind-set from "those poor kids" to "our gifted kids." Stop thinking *remediation* and start thinking *enrichment*. The enrichment mind-set means fostering intellectual curiosity, emotional engagement, and social bonding. An enriched learning environment offers challenging, complex curriculum and instruction, provides the lowest-performing students with the most highly qualified teachers, minimizes stressors, boosts participation in physical activity and the arts, ensures that students get good nutrition, and provides students with the support they need to reach high expectations. Essentially, the enrichment mind-set means maximizing students' and staff members' potential, whatever it takes. Whether or not students choose to go to college, enrichment programs prepare them to succeed in life.

Theory and Research

A study by Poplin and Soto-Hinman (2006) looked at teachers who had the highest performance rates in high-poverty schools that had not yet achieved high-performing status. These researchers found that the teachers with the highest scores used direct instruction in an engaging, well-paced, respectful but demanding format. Teachers need to express high expectations and provide the support to go with them, collaboratively use assessment data to guide professional decisions, and create caring environments.

Regardless of the approach, your teachers are the key components. It is crucial to assign the right students to the right teachers. One study (Sanders & Rivers, 1996) tracked student progress over three years and found that low-achieving students taught by the least effective teachers gained an average of 14 percentile points, whereas low-achieving students taught by the most effective teachers gained an average of 53 percentile points. As teacher effectiveness increased, lower-achieving students were first to benefit, followed by average students and, finally, by students considerably above average. Students under the tutelage of the least effective teachers made unsatisfactory gains. It is therefore essential for administrators to develop and implement strategies that lead to improved teacher effectiveness. Conduct formative teacher evaluation in conjunction with professional development. As a first step, make sure teachers use all available indicators of student academic growth to enable them to identify their own relative strengths and weaknesses.

High-Poverty Schools Making It Happen

At Esparza Elementary in San Antonio, Texas, principal Melva Matkin acknowledges to parents and staff that the school's students lack many of the benefits of a middle-class upbringing. But instead of bemoaning the situation, the school staff provides after-school enrichment activities, such as guitar or violin lessons, archery, chess, ballet folklórico, technology, and journalism. In addition, her school provides more field trips and real-life experiences than do other, more affluent schools. The school's prevailing attitude is "Because our students have less, we must provide more."

Enrichment on a schoolwide level reflects a broad commitment to the school's mission and has a dramatic impact on student performance. Schools like Esparza are driven by an unshakable faith in the rightness and even the urgency of their work. This mind-set permeates the school at every level and affects decision making, hiring practices, staff development, funding, and public relations. Principals are valued as instructional leaders, and staff members dedicate themselves to continuous improvement by using data to drive their teaching, valuing professional learning, and embracing personal accountability.

Action Steps

Create a strong environmental message. Pleasant scenery, greenery, and natural settings in the classroom, school, and campus can provide a welcome respite for students and reduce mental fatigue.

- Initiate a student project to spruce up the school environment by planting trees, bushes, flowers, or a vegetable garden.
- Encourage teachers to conduct some of their lessons outdoors, in a nearby park or under a tree.
- Never allow graffiti to remain on school walls, lockers, or any other surface.
- If possible, let fresh air into your rooms.
- Put up stress-relieving posters or murals of natural settings.
- Bring plants and flowers into the classroom to relieve an otherwise dreary setting and reinvigorate your students.
- Allow classes to adopt sections of the school (e.g., "This hallway is managed by Mr. Robbins's class").

Create a staffwide enrichment mind-set. Many of your students will have undiagnosed stress disorders (e.g., reactive attachment disorder, depression, generalized anxiety disorder, post-traumatic stress disorder, or learned helplessness) or learning delays (e.g., dyscalculia or dyslexia). For many, an Individualized Education Plan is appropriate. The IEP should be created by a team of people who know the student best, including at least one parent or guardian, a school counselor, a special education teacher, and the teacher most involved with the student. The IEP should outline student strengths and weaknesses and set a plan in motion, including clear, measurable goals for weekly, monthly, and annual checkpoints. To match student progress with these goals, you'll need a wide variety of data to establish benchmarks. The process should begin in staff meetings and end in the classroom. On a general note, set the bar high with an attitude of "enrich like crazy" by

- Communicating a strong message to staff that every level of student achievement, however low or high, should be considered the floor, not the ceiling.
- Insisting that staff members talk to kids about career opportunities that stretch their imaginations.
- Holding book drives among your staff, asking teachers to bring in books to donate to students, to get enriching materials into kids' homes.
- Getting away from the drill-and-kill mind-set and moving toward fresh, engaged learning.

Always look for one more enriching edge. Many schools ensure that no opportunity to create an enriching experience is wasted. KIPP academies have extended school days and years, for example. Months away from school-ing hurt, so many schools wisely get their low-SES students into extensive summer programs. In addition, a large and compelling body of research suggests that nutrition plays a major role in cognition, memory, mood, and behavior. Nutritional status is strongly correlated with a host of family and environmental variables—including socioeconomic status—likely to affect neurocognitive development. Studies have shown that food insecurity—which is more prevalent among low-SES children—has a deleterious effect on students' reading skills and mathematical performance (Jyoti, Frongillo, & Jones, 2005). An essential point to note is that the *quantity* of food low-SES children get isn't the problem so much as the *quality* of the food. In fact, dietary restriction (20–30 percent less quantity) is good for learning: recent research suggests that dietary restriction increases the production of new brain cells (Levenson & Rich, 2007). Chronic stress—which, as we know, is a key risk factor among low-SES populations—may also steer the diet in a more unhealthy direction, thereby contributing to long-term disease risk (Cartwright et al., 2003). High stress is associated with high consumption of fatty foods, low consumption of fruits and vegetables, and a greater likeli-hood of snacking and skipping breakfast. Two good books to consult on this subject include *Brain Foods for Kids* by Nicola Graimes and, for your staff,

The Edge Effect by Eric Braverman. You may also want to initiate a school-wide effort to inform parents that taking care of their children means giving them high-quality food, not a high quantity of substandard food. In the meantime, your school can

- Begin to order cafeteria foods that are more healthful (and thus brain-friendly) and reduce the availability of foods of marginal value (e.g., fatty, starchy, and sugary foods).
- Post information about how different foods affect the brain (e.g., "Proteins help the brain stay alert").
- Get kids involved in science projects that assess the nutritional value of various foods.

Enrichment programs can be implemented through three types of approaches: top-down, bottom-up, or a combination of the two. The top-down approach means that policymakers, administrators, or executives are mandating and supporting enrichment efforts. The bottom-up implementation means that the real doers (teachers, child care providers, and parents) begin taking actions unilaterally, regardless of the "official" policy. The combination approach means that while the "doers" are taking immediate action to maximize possibilities, additional efforts are in progress to affect public policy. As a rule, the combination approach is most effective because it is more comprehensive and pervasive.

Seven Achievement Killers: Mistakes That High-Performing Schools Never Make

We have unpacked the positive schoolwide strategies; now it's time to look at what *doesn't* work. Although it's true that every school staff has to find its own particular path to success, here are seven across-the-board "success killers" to avoid.

Mistake #1: Overdoing the Pep Talks and Hot Air

Avoid the rah-rah speeches about how we all can and should do better. Instead of repeating platitudes, explain *why* hope is justified. Talk about *what* will happen, *when* it will happen, and *how* it will happen. The planning process is relevant only when the staff that's doing the planning is buying into the change. If the staff isn't buying, the change won't happen. Administrators can effect change by sharing a clear, coherent vision of hope that is supported by doable, budgeted steps. Communicate to your staff key dates and benchmarks for the improvement effort; the specific action steps to be taken; the specific sources of time, money, and human capital; clear objectives for everyone; and confident, genuine excitement.

Mistake #2: Planning Endlessly

Avoid thinking that the more you plan and the more paperwork you generate, the better your plan will be. Don't fool yourself into thinking that the more time you spend getting the plan right, the fewer mistakes your plan will have. You will make mistakes; get over it. Just keep them inexpensive, learn from them, and move on. If you cannot generate, share, and agree upon a plan in 30 days, the plan is too complicated. If your plan is more than 10 pages long, condense it. Your plan needs to decide what changes, if any, your school needs to make in the following areas:

- Physical environment.
- Morale and attitude.
- Data collection and management.
- Policymaking.
- Staff recruitment and development.
- Classroom engagement strategies.
- Instructional practices and academic enrichment.
- Student support services.

Your plan should assign responsibilities to staff members, communicate when staff teams will be assembled, and specify how ongoing data collection and morale building will be addressed.

Mistake #3: Putting Kids First and Staff Last

An essential part of the formula for success is getting your staff on board, collectively, to buy into the new paradigm of change. Put staff first on your list of priorities, because teacher quality matters (Jordan, Mendro, & Weerasinghe, 1997). Of course, we all want to find and keep good teachers, but we should also continually upgrade their skills and assign the best teachers to the kids who struggle the most. Reward those highly effective staff members to stay on.

Like soldiers in war, teachers need logistical support (e.g., classroom supplies), emotional support (e.g., a willing ear, an open door, and flexible accommodations), and development (e.g., training in new instructional strategies).

There's no way to sugarcoat this: it takes money to bring in high-quality people for the long haul. You'll need to sharpen your proposal-writing skills for getting funding to support better staff development, for example. In the meantime, your staff needs to feel they are supported by the administration. There are many ways to do that, including

- Giving short but sincere compliments.
- Visiting classrooms and pointing out positives.
- Brainstorming with other staff members and following up on how the staff has (or has not) implemented the ideas.
- Providing a steady hand and being a dependable listener.
- Paying attention to and taking steps to resolve such teacher issues as stress, lack of planning time, lack of collegiality, and so on.
- Helping staff to form study groups with this book.
- Taking over a teacher's classroom while he or she observes a highly effective teacher's class.

Finally, give teachers the time they need for destressing, debriefing, and collaborating. Excellence takes time. You cannot expect your staff to get results in a high-stakes, challenging job with no planning time. That's like asking an actress to perform without giving her a chance to read the script or walk through her lines. You'll never get the quality you need by cutting corners. Each school needs to find its own way to carve out this time; for example, you could have teachers meet 45 minutes before or after school once every week or two, designate monthly early dismissal days, have rotating substitute teachers take over classes while teachers meet, or have half a teacher team take charge of the kids for the entire team while the other half meets.

Mistake #4: Creating a Climate of Fear

Teachers work best when they feel free to make "errors of enthusiasm." Your staff needs leeway to try out new things, to take risks with students and step outside the box now and then. If the administrative climate imposed is that of desperation and fear, you're not likely to get results. Your staff can be professional but still have a sense of humor and enjoy staff celebrations. Teaching well is a tough job, and expecting teachers to be locked in on test scores on a daily basis is unreasonable. Keep the climate focused on the overarching mission and cut teachers slack when needed.

Melva Matkin, the principal of Esparza Elementary in San Antonio, Texas, does everything she can to avoid the "fear mentality" but acknowledges that it's tough. The district and statewide focus on testing really challenges her staff. Teachers sometimes end up in a mode of compliance ("Just tell me what to do, and I'll do it!") rather than a mode of creativity, innovation, and risk taking. Many are afraid to veer too far from the materials provided or to step back far enough from the situation to get a broad perspective of what the students need to know. Every year, her challenge as principal is to help teachers get a bigger picture of what they *really* need to do. She provides them with support and encouragement to do what is both fun and right for kids. Her approach seems to be paying off: Esparza has received a Governor's Educator Excellence Award and been designated a Texas Blue Ribbon School, a National Blue Ribbon School of Excellence, a Title I Distinguished School, and a Texas Recognized School. Matkin has clearly been able to avoid the mistake of using fear to "motivate" staff. Give teachers the tools and the "why," and support them to do their job.

Mistake #5: Measuring Improvement Solely Through Test Scores

Top schools understand and work with the standards because they are the public, mainstream measures of a school's success. When test scores go up, morale goes up. But when you focus only on the measurable tangibles, like your test score data, you'll miss out on some other, equally important data. The "vibes" at your school may not be measurable, but you can sure feel them. Trust your intuition as well as the hard data. "Soft" signs of a successful school include

- Teachers and students socializing and helping one another out.
- High levels of school spirit among students and staff.
- Teachers who show affection toward students and one another.

- Smiles on kids' and adults' faces as they walk around campus.
- Small celebrations.
- Fewer fights and upsets.
- Better social skills among students.

Another problem with focusing purely on test scores is that it actually takes your focus away from long-term improvement. According to former superintendent and current consultant Ron Fitzgerald, all school leaders ought to be able to agree to each of these statements:

1. Your school has staff task forces that design, maintain, and improve school programs, policies, and procedures.
2. Your school district, and each school in the district, has drafted a mission statement approved by the school board.
3. Each school and teacher in the district uses concept models to guide actions and evaluations under the mission statement.
4. Each school and teacher in the district pays strong attention to research on brain-friendly teaching.
5. Each school's annual professional growth activities are focused on improving the staff's application of its defined concept models as well as on such areas as new state requirements and new health and safety concerns.
6. Each teacher uses formative assessment data to improve learning results.

Mistake #6: Treating the Symptoms, Not the Causes

Aspirin might make your headache go away temporarily. But if your lifestyle or workplace continually generates stressful situations, the headache's just going to come back. When faced with a problem, it's important to treat the causes rather than the symptoms. For example, if kids in your school have deficits in reading fluency, a reading program may address the problem, but making more books available for kids to take home could address the source of the problem. Similarly, adding any new discipline program may help improve student behavior, but the good ones (e.g., Conscious Discipline or Love and Logic) *meet needs to reduce the need* for kids to act out. Just increasing classroom engagement may reduce many discipline issues permanently. In fact, at some schools, implementing a heavy-handed discipline program may undermine your progress. If kids act out because of cultural differences, consider implementing a diversity program to personally involve them in the content. If kids behave poorly out of boredom, the only way you'll solve the problem is to use strategies that actively engage students. If kids feel disconnected, strengthen relationships through mentoring, clubs, team-building exercises, and community activities. Whatever you do, avoid wasting precious time, money, teacher morale, and emotional energy on "solutions" that only treat the symptoms.

Mistake #7: Counting On Big Wins Quickly

Some schools begin their turnaround process with 20, 30, or even 50 goals. That's not going to happen in a school year. Improvement is not a race; it's not even a marathon. It is the process of life. Don't waste time on grand plans; instead, focus on immediate micro changes. The big changes will happen, but they'll take time (Felner et al., 1997). Start looking for and celebrating the daily practices that will eventually turn the tide. At your school, you can

- Set manageable daily, weekly, and monthly goals, and stick to them.
- Make one small change each week and practice it until it's second nature.
- Make one big change each month and practice it until it's second nature.
- Add stress-reducing activities, paint and clean up the classrooms, increase available light, and make any other small modifications that will improve student performance and morale.
- Celebrate progress and set new goals.

Moving Forward Together

Let's say you're an administrator taking over a high school in Baltimore, Maryland, that has a bad reputation as low-performing and wildly undisciplined. Let's say your goals are to (1) increase attendance, (2) decrease dropout rates, (3) triple the rate of promotion from 9th to 10th grade, and (4) get a 28-point increase in the number of students passing the state math test. How would you do it?

Baltimore's Patterson High School is a high-performing, high-poverty school that accomplished these goals by decreasing class size (thus building relationships and accountability); instituting career academies and a 9th grade success academy (thus providing enrichment); focusing on the future (thus providing hope); and providing extra help for students through tutoring and evening, weekend, and summer school programs (thus building the skills to upgrade students' academic operating systems). Today, this school continues to succeed.

In Hamilton County, Tennessee, the Benwood Initiative was launched after a statewide report identified nine of Hamilton County's elementary schools—all in Chattanooga—as being among the 20 lowest-achieving schools in the state. The district hired new principals for the majority of the schools, and the Public Education Fund started a principal leadership institute that taught principals to use data and to coach teachers to improve instruction. The district removed concentrations of ineffective teachers at high-poverty schools by reshuffling the teachers throughout the district. Then the new leadership implemented job-embedded professional development to improve teachers' instructional practice. Most teachers received in-class coaching, and specially selected teachers became Osborne Fellows, a status that entitled them to full scholarships in master's degree programs customized to fit the needs of the district and the special challenges of urban teaching. The district also rewarded top teachers with bonuses. In the 2004–2005 school year, 53 percent of Benwood 3rd graders scored at the Advanced or Proficient level in reading on the Tennessee Comprehensive Assessment Program; in 2007, 80 percent scored at that level (Chenoweth, 2007).

What do the schools profiled in this book have in common? They have all done more than talk about change and make plans for change. They set themselves apart by actually rolling up their sleeves to *be the change*. There was no waiting for a miracle; the staff collectively chose to *be the miracle*.

A telltale sign of a low-performing school is a culture of excuses. At successful schools, teachers, administrators, and students are all on the same side. Like the schools profiled above, these schools build academic knowledge, social skills, and personal character through high standards, rigorous coursework, and strong relationships between teachers and students and between the school and the community. Successful schools instill substantial and realistic hope and cultivate the dreams of the next generation.

Countless schools have beaten the odds stacked against them. A powerful, schoolwide approach leads to positive effects that are neither transient nor localized. Such an approach enables you to focus on the priorities that will give you the biggest return on your investment of precious time, money, and human capital. To become a turnaround school, you need to isolate the important factors for change and focus relentlessly on them. In Chapter 5, I examine how you can implement specific changes at the classroom level.

5

Classroom-Level Success Factors

Mr. Hawkins is starting to see a glimmer of hope. He has learned that his students' cognitive capacity can be improved, and he has been introduced to some schools that have achieved success with the students he used to refer to as "those kids." But now he's feeling a new and different pressure. The focus is turning to the classroom—specifically, his classroom. He asks himself a new question that he has never thought of before: "Do I have what it takes to succeed at working with kids from poverty?" Just asking this question was a breakthrough for him. He is starting to see "those kids" as "our kids" and is embarking on the most important journey of all, reflection. He now thinks, "I wonder if I can get good enough before retirement—it's less than six years away."

Five SHARE Factors for Classrooms

In Chapter 4, we looked at schools that effected positive, widespread change. Now let's take a look at improvement from the classroom perspective. The more you examine the research, the greater the perspectives offered. All researchers (including myself) have biases based on their own life experiences. There are differences in the philosophy of instruction, for example: some believe that good curriculum is the key, while those who are handed a prepackaged, standardized curriculum may find that empowering students to discover meaning will better serve them over the long haul. Some believe that classroom discipline should underpin good instruction, whereas others believe that strong emotional engagement all but erases discipline problems. The list of classroom factors that make a difference is potentially huge. Here is a list of research I have consulted in building my own list of essential classroom factors:

- *A "Teacher's Dozen": Fourteen General, Research-Based Principles for Improving Higher Learning in Our Classrooms* (Angelo, 1993)
- *Principals and Student Achievement* (Cotton, 2003)
- *Teaching with the Brain in Mind* (Jensen, 2005)
- *Classroom Instruction That Works* (Marzano, Pickering, & Pollock, 2001)
- *The Art and Science of Teaching* (Marzano, 2007)
- *Teaching What Matters Most: Standards and Strategies for Raising Student Achievement* (Strong, Silver, & Perini, 2001)
- *Twelve Principles of Effective Teaching and Learning for Which There Is Substantial Empirical Support* (Tiberius & Tipping, 1990)

The best way to launch an improvement effort is to increase the odds of success with the factor you have the most influence over: the quality of teaching in your school. If your staff is already reasonably skilled, what will make a difference with kids living in poverty? That's the focus of this chapter. My takeaway message is simple: it's not how much you do; it's what you do, and for how long. I considered both the research listed above and what we know about the effects of poverty to arrive at the instructional strategies that I believe matter most.

Five themes emerge from the research as drivers of change. Of course, none of these themes exists in a vacuum, and they are all influenced by the systemic factors discussed in Chapter 4. Nonetheless, the classroom is ground zero—the place where all these forces converge either to compel success or to allow failure. Here, supported by the research and the schools that make them happen, are the classroom-level *SHARE* factors:

- **S**tandards-Based Curriculum and Instruction.
- **H**ope Building.
- **A**rts, Athletics, and Advanced Placement.
- **R**etooling of the Operating System.
- **E**ngaging Instruction.

Standards-Based Curriculum and Instruction

As we have seen, a multitude of factors influence low-SES students' success in school: support of the whole child, hard data, accountability, relationship building, and an enrichment mind-set. Unfortunately, the overall speed of implementation of change in schools teaching students from poverty has been agonizingly slow, and many of the outcomes are subjective and incremental. In the final analysis, test scores are still where the rubber meets the road: they are the most noticeable marker by which educators are judged. And the way to improve test scores is to align curriculum and instruction with state standards.

Theory and Research

For most schools teaching students in poverty, meeting the standards is a bit like trying to nail Jell-O to a tree. The effects of standards on these schools have been well studied, and the standards rarely match up with good instruction. Assessment expert James Popham (2004) says, "Forget it—the standard achievement test makers have *no interest* in selecting test items that will reflect effective instruction" (p. 46). Standardized tests require fine-grained contrasts, meaning that test makers get very few questions to distinguish minor skill and knowledge contrasts among students. Those contrasts create score spread, which must be produced by just an hour or two of testing, so test items must have a wide range of difficulty.

Which testing items produce the widest spread? According to Popham, it's those that are most closely linked to socioeconomic status. Popham found that anywhere from 15 to 80 percent of questions (depending on the subject area being tested) on norm-referenced standardized achievement tests were SES-linked. Therefore, because students' socioeconomic status is out of the control of school officials, there will always be a testing gap. He suggests that we all learn a bit more about assessment and start adopting instruments that actually measure what we're teaching. Tests ought to include fewer and more general items and should give teachers more specific feedback so that they can actually improve instruction.

Having said that, standards are here to stay for the foreseeable future, and your school still needs to pay attention to them. Standards-based reform has actually had a few positive effects on student achievement (Gamoran, 2007). In addition, closer adherence to standards improves teacher focus, and that correlates with improved teacher quality at low-income schools (Desimone, Smith, Hayes, & Frisvold, 2005). Standards have helped to

- Expose social inequities in school performance—schools must report test results separately for students in different demographic subgroups.
- Obtain better opportunities for disadvantaged students—schools not achieving adequate yearly progress receive transfers and supplemental services.
- Improve opportunities for disadvantaged students—No Child Left Behind requires districts to place a "highly qualified teacher" in every classroom.
- Promote curricula and teaching methods for which there is scientific evidence of success.
- Put everyone on the same page at each grade level, no matter what school you are at.

Of course, standards alone are not enough, but they are an important component in helping to turn around low-performing schools. Although standards may not be the most accurate long-term measure, they still matter to many primary stakeholders: parents, policymakers, voters, and teachers. The reason top schools focus on standards is simple: for many, it is the most visible measure of a school's success. One of the reasons for their value may be survival: staff members are practically forced to work together toward a meaningful goal. Improved schools vertically align their curricula to articulate with state standards and assessments. Although you'll use multiple measures to assess your students' performance, remember that the standards are still in the magnified center of the public's attention span.

High-Poverty Schools Making It Happen

Let's examine a high-performing school whose emphasis on the standards has led to significant improvement. North Star Academy in New Jersey serves 384 students, 99 percent of whom are minorities and 90 percent of whom receive free or reduced-price lunch. Its graduation rate is nearly 100 percent. One hundred percent of North Star's 12th grade general education students pass the New Jersey High School Statewide Assessment, compared with 44.2 percent of students in the Newark school district and 19.5 percent of students from nearby neighborhood schools. North Star has the highest rate of four-year college acceptance and attendance of any school in the state of New Jersey, regardless of socioeconomic level.

What's the secret of North Star's accomplishment? The school's most innovative features are the level of personalization it provides and its commitment to ensuring student mastery of the content standards. The school has developed a set of interim assessments, aligned with the curriculum and state standards, that it administers every six to eight weeks to help teachers understand student needs. Teachers receive the results in an easy-to-read spreadsheet. In addition, the school's assistant principals and lead teachers do a daily walk-through of the school, visiting at least 85 percent of the classrooms and providing informal feedback.

With the data from these observations and from the interim student assessments, teachers use the North Star Assessment Analysis Sheet and Instruction Plan template to draw connections between their instruction and student performance and to decide what they need to do to help students master the standards. The teacher and the department analyze results to identify which students or groups of students did not learn the standard and therefore need additional instruction, whether through small-group work, tutoring, or acceleration. Teachers develop plans to differentiate instruction, supplemented by other forms of support that help students perform to the level of the standards. Teachers receive training in the data management programs that are used to organize the student assessment data and then determine instructional groupings. If a student is not doing well, his or her teacher immediately asks the question "How can I teach this differently, and what needs to change so that the student will achieve mastery?"

Action Steps

Turn standards into meaningful units. The overall standards need to be broken down into daily objectives. You'll need to do some additional work to translate them into meaningful teaching units. Within your school district's curriculum, your staff will need to customize thematically. Here's how:

1. Take the time to identify core concepts, skills, and essential questions that go together. Use Wiggins and McTighe's book *Understanding by Design* (2005) as a guide to take the lessons and units and create essential questions that address the big picture of each objective.

2. "Chunk" similar objectives together within units to make units more meaningful and to enable students to retain the important concepts. You might even create an overall theme for your units.

3. Help students see the patterns within the content and skills being taught; resist just teaching scattered, unrelated objectives. Teaching thematically related information enables better neural network connection.

4. Create questions as a guide through the objectives and units, so that students' brains are able to focus on the more important points within lessons and units. I recommend making these questions open-ended and higher-level. The questions can even be so general that they become the focus of the whole unit (in effect, these would be essential questions).

5. When you create the detailed objectives for each unit, remember that they must include the specific content covered plus a challenging verb of action. It's not uncommon for teachers to write something like "American Indians" in their lesson-planning books, but this is not an objective; it's a topic. What exactly will students know and be able to do and connect with after this lesson? Ask yourself this question while writing the objective that will be assessed at the end of the lesson or unit.

Pre-assess to determine students' background knowledge. Even if you already have a good idea of what you want to teach, this step will allow you to make an immediate customized lesson.

1. Create pre-tests containing a combination of fill-in-the-blank, short-answer, and multiple-choice questions.

2. Ensure that the questions represent the key concepts and skills that will be taught in the upcoming unit.

3. Write out a half-dozen questions for each lesson objective, and subdivide them cleanly. That way, you'll be better able to ascertain students' level of understanding of each lesson objective.

4. Add a few edgy or provocative "teaser" questions that prime students' interest in the upcoming unit.

5. Give the unit pre-test about one week before starting the unit to ensure that you have plenty of time to adjust your lessons according to students' background knowledge.

Adjust your lesson plans. Adjust your daily lessons according to the pre-assessment results. You'll want to

- Know where to begin the unit or lesson, depending on students' background knowledge.
- Note student misconceptions before the unit.
- Know how long you might need to spend on a certain concept.
- Know how to sequence your objectives for the unit.
- Know how to group students.
- Know how to prime the students' brains for what is coming up in the unit.
- Show students the conceptual "chunks" in the unit through a mind map, graphic organizer, or concept web.
- Know how to decide which students you might be able to exempt from the unit to work on more challenging unit-related projects (known as curriculum compacting).
- Be able to find "experts" in the classroom.
- Compare students' knowledge before and after the lesson or unit.

Hope Building

We have expectations of all kids, but sometimes we expect too little—especially of children raised in poverty. We assume that low-SES students will have less access to resources, be more stressed, be sick more often, and have less emotional support and intellectual stimulation at home. However, the likely conclusion—the one that says that children of poverty will necessarily do poorly in school—should not be automatic. Although it has statistical support, it does not have to be true. Why?

Because teacher beliefs and assumptions play a big part in the outcome, *especially* for students subjected to low expectations. These students have experienced enough negatives in their lives and often feel hopeless and see no viable future for themselves. More than any other school population, they need a megadose of hope. Hope changes brain chemistry, which influences the decisions we make and the actions we take. Hopefulness must be pervasive, and every single student should be able to feel it, see it, and hear it daily.

Theory and Research

One possible and dire consequence of unrelenting hopelessness is learned helplessness, which is *not* a genetic phenomenon but an adaptive response to life conditions. As I discussed in Chapter 2, this is a well-studied (Peterson, Maier, & Seligman, 1995) and chronic condition. Students with learned helplessness believe that they have no control over their situations and that whatever they do is futile. Because of these persistent feelings of inadequacy, individuals will remain passive even when they actually have the power to change their circumstances. Such beliefs and behaviors can take hold as early as 1st grade. Many kids with learned helplessness become fatalistic about their lives, and they're more likely to drop out of school or become pregnant while in their teens.

Hope and learned optimism are crucial factors in turning low-SES students into high achievers. Far from being some wistful ideal, hope, like other powerful positive emotions, may trigger change through enhanced metabolic states like physical activity and by influencing brain-changing gene expression (Jiaxu & Weiyi, 2000). Hopeful kids try harder, persist longer, and ultimately get better grades. When educators believe students are competent, students tend to perform better; conversely, when educators believe students have deficits, students tend to perform more poorly (Johns, Schmader, & Martens, 2005). One study (Zohar, Degani, & Vaaknin, 2001) found that 49 percent of teachers surveyed considered higher-order thinking "inappropriate" for poor or low-achieving students. It becomes a self-fulfilling prophecy: expect less, get less, lose hope—and the cycle continues.

High-Poverty Schools Making It Happen

How much difference does hope really make? The student body at Burgess Elementary School in Atlanta, Georgia, is 99 percent African American, with 81 percent qualifying for free or reduced-price lunch. After instituting a program that educated stakeholders on standards, heightened parental involvement, built strong community partnerships, and enhanced emotional connections among parents, students, and teachers, Burgess went from

29 percent above the national norm in reading and 34 percent in math to 64 percent above the national norm in reading and 72 percent in math. High hopes and the enrichment, support, and strong relationships stemming from those hopes made all the difference.

In an experiment at Oak Elementary School (a pseudonym), researchers Rosenthal and Jacobson (1992) administered an intelligence test to all students at the beginning of the school year. Then they randomly selected 20 percent of the students—independent of their test results—and reported to the teachers that these students were showing "unusual potential for intellectual growth" and could be expected to "bloom" in their academic performance by the end of the year. Eight months later, at the end of the academic year, the researchers came back and retested all the students. Students labeled as "intelligent" showed significant improvement in test performance over those who were not singled out for the teachers' attention. As the researchers noted, the change in teachers' expectations of these "special" children had led to an actual change in the children's performance. For ethical reasons, the Oak Elementary experiment focused only on favorable or positive expectations' impact on intellectual competence, but it is reasonable to infer that unfavorable expectations could lead to a corresponding decrease in performance.

Action Steps

Could your staff have expectations that are too low? Could your students be missing out on a more challenging curriculum because of teacher bias? These steps will help you find out.

Inventory students and staff. Find out the level of hope or hopelessness among your students. Create and administer a simple 25-question survey for students asking such questions as

1. What is the likelihood of your succeeding in school and graduating?
   (a) Not good.
   (b) Hard to tell.
   (c) Excellent.
2. How much support do you feel you get from your teachers in your schoolwork and personal life?

(a) Not much.

(b) Some.

(c) Plenty.

3. When you think about where you'll be 10 or 20 years from now, what comes to mind?

(a) Uncertainty.

(b) Some good and some bad.

(c) Mostly good things.

Now create and administer a simple 25-question survey asking staff members how often they use certain strategies (without labeling them as "hope builders"):

1. How often do you find yourself telling success stories of past students or famous people that students might be able to relate to?

(a) That's not my style.

(b) Occasionally.

(c) Several times a week.

2. Do you use affirmations and celebrate learning milestones?

(a) That's not my style.

(b) Occasionally.

(c) Several times a week.

3. How often do you use positive, optimistic language with your students (e.g., "You've got a great gift!" or "I love how you did that! Where did you come up with that idea?" or "I know you haven't done well, but I'm on your side and I know how to get you where you want to go.")?

(a) That's not my style.

(b) Occasionally.

(c) Several times a week.

Implement 24/7 hope. There has been a good deal of research on the power of hope and optimism. A pioneer is Martin Seligman, also known as the "father of positive psychology." His research (Seligman & Csikszent-mihalyi, 2000) suggests that hopefulness can be taught; in fact, there is a popular university-level curriculum that teaches *positive states*—what they are and how to prolong them; *an engaged life*—the value of participation, not passivity; and *a meaningful life*—how to focus on the things that matter most and get outside yourself with service work and volunteering. Other strategies that build hope include

- Using daily affirmations (both verbally stated and posted on walls).
- Asking to hear students' hopes and offering reinforcement of those hopes.
- Telling students specifically why they can succeed.
- Providing needed academic resources (e.g., paper and pencils, computer time).
- Helping students to set goals and build goal-getting skills.
- Telling true stories of hope about people to whom students can relate.
- Offering help, encouragement, and caring as often as needed.
- Teaching students life skills in small daily chunks.
- Avoiding complaining about students' deficits. If they don't have it, teach it!
- Treating all the kids in your class as potentially gifted.
- Building academic, emotional, and social assets in students.

Do not interpret hope as a pie-in-the-sky or Pollyanna attitude. Hope changes brain chemistry, which influences behaviors. Spreading hope does not mean giving students a thoughtless pep talk to the tune of "You can be a doctor, an astronaut, or the next U.S. president in three easy steps!" What you must say to your students is this: "You have your dreams, and that's a good start. Be persistent and work hard. We're on your side, and we'll do everything we can to help you succeed. Go for it!" Ask staff members to make an index card of each hope-building strategy or to post the list on the classroom's back wall. Implement a strategy until it becomes second nature and the classroom is filled with hope.

Monitor results. You'll want to get readings on the implementation of hopefulness at your school:

- Administer the 25-question survey mentioned above twice a year to get a reading from students.
- Take informal walks around campus and make short visits to classrooms. You should see kids who smile and talk with other students and teachers.

- Look for a spirit of volunteerism. Optimistic kids volunteer for projects, services, and mentoring.
- Ask staff to keep track of random acts of kindness and hopeful activities. You see kids for just 30 hours a week; you cannot afford to give them a bad day.

Here is a true story demonstrating the power of hope. Monty was a poor 16-year-old student growing up in the rural agricultural region of Salinas, California. When asked to write a "dreams" essay in high school about his life after graduation, he wrote about running a huge ranch and raising thoroughbred horses. A few days later, his teacher returned the graded essays. To his shock, Monty received an F. He asked his teacher, "How can I get an F on my dreams?" The teacher replied, "Because I asked you to be practical, and you were not practical." Monty stared in disbelief. The teacher, realizing his emotional state, added, "However, if you'd like to rewrite the paper and make your dreams more practical, I'll let you do that so you can raise your grade." Monty collected himself and looked the teacher in the eye. "Miss, you can keep your F; I'll keep my dreams." And in the end, Monty did reach his dreams. He owns a large thoroughbred ranch, has trained horses for the Queen of England, has written five bestselling books, and was the subject of a major motion picture. Monty Roberts is the original "horse whisperer."

Monty grew up in generational poverty; all he had were his hopes and dreams. Dreams mobilize your students. If you do nothing else, provide hope for the future. For many people living in poverty, hope and faith in tomorrow are the only things that keep them going each day. Every member of your staff must buy into this fact: if brains can change for the worse because of hopelessness, they can change for the better because of the hope provided by good people in a good school. For students living in poverty, hope is not a frivolous luxury but an absolute necessity.

Arts, Athletics, and Advanced Placement

The "old-school" way of thinking is that kids with less background knowledge need a slower-paced or dumbed-down curriculum. But that myth has been debunked (Marzano, 2004): there are specific strategies that can help build the background knowledge needed for success. Many educators have tried and failed at raising expectations permanently. When students don't immediately meet the new higher expectations, these teachers say, "See, I knew it. They just can't do it." But no curriculum, instruction, or assessment should be considered in a vacuum. You can't raise expectations without also raising students' learning capacity. High-performing high-poverty schools not only add complex, challenging curriculum—including the arts, athletics, and advanced placement classes—but also add capacity to each student.

Theory and Research

Before low-SES kids even get to school, they have been subjected to years of doing without. As we saw in Chapter 2, poor children are half as likely to be taken to museums, theaters, or the library and are less likely to go on other culturally enriching outings (Bradley & Corwyn, 2002). They have fewer or smaller designated play areas in the home and spend more time watching television and less time exercising than well-off children do (Evans, 2004). Financial limitations often exclude low-SES kids from healthy after-school activities, such as music, athletics, dance, or drama (Bracey, 2006). The arts and a challenging curriculum enhance essential learning skills and cognition, whereas sports, recess, and physical activity increase neurogenesis and reduce kids' chances for depression. Therefore, it is in our own best interest to incorporate the arts, athletic activity, and advanced placement curriculum into the school day.

The enriching and engaging arts. The arts are an oft-neglected area of the curriculum that have a dramatic impact on student performance. The arts can build attentional skills (Posner, Rothbart, Sheese, & Kieras, 2008); develop processing skills, such as sequencing and manipulation of procedures and data (Jonides, 2008); strengthen memory skills, especially short-term memory (Chan et al., 1998); and build lifelong, transferable skills, such as reading (Wandell, Dougherty, Ben-Shachar, & Deutsch, 2008). Theater, drama, and other performance arts foster participants' emotional intelligence, timing, reflection, and respect for diversity; build memorization and processing skills; and help students win social status and friends (Gazzaniga et al., 2008). Studying the arts also correlates with higher SAT scores: compared with those taking no arts courses, students taking theater and drama scored higher on the widely used college entrance test (visit http://old.menc.org/information/advocate/sat.html for details).

UCLA professor of education James Catterall (Catterall, Chapleau, & Iwanaga, 1999) analyzed data on more than 25,000 students from the National Educational Longitudinal Survey to determine how engagement in the arts relates to student performance and attitudes. He found that students with high levels of arts participation outperform "arts-poor" students on virtually every measure and that high arts participation makes a more significant difference to low-income students than to high-income students. In addition, Catterall documented the difference between low-SES students who took music lessons in grades 8–12 and comparable students who took no music lessons and found that the former not only significantly increased their math scores but also improved their reading, history, and geography scores by 40 percent. Integration of music in the curriculum can contribute to better academic performance and enhanced neurobiological development. If you scan the brains of musically inexperienced children, give them 15 weeks of piano lessons, and then scan their brains again, you'll see physical changes (Stewart et al., 2003).

Training in the arts influences cognition because participants become motivated to practice their particular art with intentional, focused determination. This motivation typically leads to sustained attention, which leads to greater efficiency of the brain network involved in attention. That improved attention in turn leads to cognitive improvement in many areas, including math and science (Spelke, 2008), according to the results of a three-year collaboration between the Dana Consortium on Arts and Cognition and more than a dozen neuroscientists from five universities (Gazzaniga, 2008). For the first time, we are seeing that we can teach transferable skills that may raise students' practical or "fluid" intelligence (Jaeggi et al., 2008). In fact, the implicit learning that the arts provide transfers better than the explicit "textbook" learning of many other subjects. Arts build your students' academic operating systems as well as or better than anything else your school offers. To put it bluntly, if you do not have a strong arts program, what are you replacing it with?

Athletics that advance academics. Physical education and athletics are another aspect of school not commonly associated with improved cognition.

But in addition to improving students' health, cardiovascular capacity, muscle strength, body coordination, speed, reaction times, and stress responses, athletics enhance cognition (Sibley & Etnier, 2003), academic outcomes (Pellegrini & Bohn, 2005), and graduation rates, and they reduce behavioral problems (Newman, 2005). Schools that cut physical education time in favor of more "sit-and-git" test prep are missing out on big academic gains.

Exercise increases the release of *brain-derived neurotrophic factor* (BDNF), a protein that supports learning and memory function, repair and maintenance of neural circuits, and the production of brain cells that are crucial to forming the connections the brain needs to learn. It also strengthens cells and protects them from dying out (Bjørnebekk, Mathé, & Brené, 2005). Fernando Gómez-Pinilla and his team at UCLA found that voluntary exercise increased levels of BDNF in the hippocampus, a brain area involved with learning and memory (Gómez-Pinilla, Dao, & So, 1997). Some studies have found strong evidence that exercise increases the production and functionality of brain cells in mammals, which are highly correlated with learning, mood, and memory (Fabel et al., 2003; van Praag, Kempermann, & Gage, 1999). One study found that joggers consistently performed better than non-joggers on learning and memory tests that required the use of the prefrontal cortex (Harada et al., 2004). In addition, exercise leads to increased levels of calcium, which is transported to the brain and enhances dopamine synthesis, making the brain sharper for both cognitive problem solving and working memory (Sutoo & Akiyama, 2003).

How does all this brain stuff translate into practice? What happens to student achievement when schools engage kids in high-quality physical education? First, it improves self-concept (Tremblay, Vitaro, & Brendgen, 2000) and reduces stress and aggression (Wagner, 1997). Second, it improves academic performance (Sallis et al., 1999). An analysis conducted by the California Department of Education showed a significant relationship between public school students' academic achievement and their physical fitness (Slater, 2003). The study matched reading and mathematics scores with the fitness scores of 353,000 5th graders, 322,000 7th graders, and 279,000 9th graders. At each of the three grade levels measured, higher fitness levels were associated with higher achievement. Exercise protects against the negative factors of stress and disabilities and diseases and enhances memory, focus, and brain function, leading to better cognition and achievement. Harvard's John Ratey (Ratey & Hagerman, 2008) notes that even moderate exercise can sharpen memory and improve cognitive function and highlights a school district study showing how the students getting the most fitness also ended up with the highest academic scores.

Research also suggests that there are structural properties of an exercise-enhanced brain that optimize learning and future changes (Bruel-Jungerman, Rampon, & Laroche, 2007)—exactly what kids from poverty need! Charles H. Hillman, an associate professor of kinesiology at the University of Illinois at Urbana-Champaign, and Darla M. Castelli assessed the physical fitness levels of 239 3rd and 5th graders from four Illinois elementary schools. Their findings, published in the *Journal of Sport & Exercise Psychology*, show that children who got good marks in aerobic fitness and body-mass index earned higher scores on state exams in reading and mathematics. That relationship held true regardless of children's socioeconomic status (Hillman, Castelli, & Buck, 2005).

Sensory motor labs are another way to help jump-start academics. Many kids, especially those from poverty, do not have the essential brain wiring for academic success. Lyelle Palmer's motor skills development program at the Minnesota Learning Resource Center gives kids the foundational sensory motor skills to build academic skills in the future. Four Title I schools in North Carolina school districts implemented Palmer's SMART (Stimulating Maturity through Accelerated Readiness Training) program. The program produced high-level foundations of readiness and early literacy mastery in more than 80 percent of students from poverty (Palmer, Giese, & DeBoer, 2008). Palmer's work suggests that the sensory motor labs increase cognitive achievement at a much greater rate than simple, boring, brain-unfriendly seatwork does. The brain's cognitive systems require strong sensory platforms. Many students do not get the necessary early childhood experiences, but these solutions help the brain catch up.

At Timberwilde Elementary, a high-poverty school in Texas, the teacher-designed motor lab serves a population of kindergartners in a school of more than 800 students. The staff set up stations that are planned, sequential, and developmental, with a variety of cross-lateral (i.e., arm and leg movements that cross over from one side of the body to the other), bilateral (e.g., climbing), and unilateral (e.g., reaching) activities. The lab started in September 2007 and ended in May 2008. Students at the University of Texas at San Antonio studying motor development helped monitor the stations. Students engaged in 30-minute sessions four days a week for the entire school year. Timberwilde physical education teacher Jill Johnstone finds that her students do more than outperform the control groups; they often jump a whole school year! She plans to publish her data soon.

A study involving 163 overweight children in Augusta, Georgia, found that the cognitive and academic benefits of exercise seem to increase with the size of the dose. For this study, a cross-disciplinary research team randomly assigned children to one of three groups. The first group engaged in 40 minutes of physical activity every day after school, the second group got a 20-minute daily workout, and the third group did not participate in any special exercise sessions. After 14 weeks, the children who made the greatest improvement, as measured by both a standardized academic test and a test measuring their level of executive function (thinking processes that involve planning, organizing, abstract thought, or self-control), were those who spent 40 minutes a day playing tag and other active games designed by the researchers. The cognitive and academic gains for the 20-minutes-a-day group were half as large (Viadero, 2008).

Advanced placement jump-starters. An advanced placement curriculum builds hope within students for a better future, challenges rather than bores, exposes academic gaps to be remedied, and develops pride, self-concept, and self-esteem. Taking just one advanced placement (AP) course exposes a student to college-level work and the accompanying emphasis on critical thinking, study skills, and increased content knowledge. In fact, AP courses are predictors of college success. In a U.S. Department of Education study, Clifford Adelman (1999) concluded that "no matter how one divides the universe of students . . . a high school curriculum of high academic intensity and quality is the factor that contributes to a student's likelihood of completing a college degree" (p. 21). As a contributing factor of college success, participation in AP courses outranked grade point average, class rank, and SAT scores (pp. 18, 25).

Another study (McCauley, 2007) tested whether taking advanced placement and dual enrollment courses influenced high school students' likelihood of graduating from a four-year college or university within six years. A total of 3,781 AP and/or dual enrollment students and 2,760 non-AP and non–dual enrollment students were included in the study. Overall, the results showed that taking an AP course was a significant factor because such courses enabled high school students to become familiar with college expectations and gain college credit. In other words, a focus on college preparation in the context of a rigorous high school curriculum demystifies the college-going experience.

AVID (Advancement Via Individual Determination) is a national school-based program for low-income and first-generation students that requires students to enroll in college-preparatory classes, receive tutoring from college students, attend sessions with guest speakers from colleges and businesses, and participate in field trips to colleges and universities. A number of prominent education researchers have studied AVID, and their conclusions have informed curricular revisions and approaches to student success (Datnow, Hubbard, & Mehan, 2002; Slavin & Calderon, 2001).

Beginning in 1989, Hugh Mehan and colleagues studied AVID programs in the San Diego Unified School District, examining numerous student records and closely studying eight AVID sites. Mehan learned that AVID graduates enroll in college at a rate two-and-one-half times greater than that of their contemporaries and that AVID coordinators redefine the role of the teacher, assisting students in navigating the "hidden curriculum" of schools (Mehan, Villanueva, Hubbard, & Lintz, 1996). He notes that the longer students stay in AVID, the more successful they are. The lessons learned through AVID and its approach to schoolwide achievement have broader implications.

High-Poverty Schools Making It Happen

Can the arts turn around your school? The Chicago Arts Partnerships in Education (CAPE) has developed an innovative arts-integrated curriculum that has produced an inspiring turnaround in student achievement at 14 high-poverty schools in the large and deeply troubled Chicago public school district. At one Chicago elementary school, 84 percent of students come from families living below the poverty line, and 30 percent do not speak English. Before arts were introduced, a measly 38 percent were reading at grade level, and only 49 percent were performing at grade level in math. A strong arts program has changed things: 60 percent of students now read at grade level, and 68 percent perform at or above grade level in math (Leroux & Grossman, 1999).

Watson Williams, a magnet school for the performing arts in Utica, New York, is another elementary school success story. Watson Williams has a student mobility rate of 22 percent, and 96 percent of its students are eligible for free or reduced-price lunch. The performing arts teachers meet with the regular education teachers to integrate key concepts and vocabulary from each subject into the performing arts curriculum and performances.

For some kids, studying the arts in school is all the enrichment they'll get. Like many National Blue Ribbon Schools, Lincoln Elementary School in Mount Vernon, New York, is fully immersed in the arts. Why? In addition to building the students' brains for academics, the arts serve as an engagement and motivation strategy. At Lincoln, the curriculum hooks kids with arts at every opportunity. "Capture them in the arts, and the academics will follow," declares Lincoln's principal, George Albano. Albano is a mentor to faculty, an instructional leader who is comfortable discussing content with teachers, and an administrator familiar with his students' accomplishments and struggles. The school is a great place to be: it offers a rich, interdisciplinary curriculum that somehow finds a way to blend literacy and jazz, physics and physical education.

In Greenville, South Carolina, the arts have transformed math classrooms. Sixth graders learn about negative and positive numbers by dancing along a number line, not filling out worksheets. After support from a Kennedy Center for the Performing Arts grant, teachers abandoned their worksheet-style teaching techniques in favor of arts-based methods. It was a big change, but student enthusiasm and achievement soared.

In Ohio, Toledo School for the Arts is another arts-oriented showcase. Although the school provides a college-preparatory curriculum with arts-based learning, its main focus is on the whole child. Staff members want students to become lifelong learners whether they head to college, to art school, or directly into work as artists.

In Augusta, Georgia, the John S. Davidson Fine Arts Magnet School is a high-performing public school teaching students in grades 6–12. In addition to a curriculum of college-preparatory and advanced placement academic courses, Davidson offers courses in visual arts, music, chorus, dance, and theater.

Finally, at Belle Isle Enterprise Middle School in Oklahoma, all students are expected to study foreign languages and participate in fine and performing arts, with periodic exhibitions and performances punctuating the school year. Fifty-nine percent of Belle Isle students are eligible for free or reduced-price lunch, yet 97–99 percent of all students achieved a rating of Proficient or above on the state tests.

Can active kids become smarter kids? Educators in Naperville District 203, a suburban district of 18,600 students just west of Chicago, put students through more than a dozen heart-pumping activities. The students wear heart monitors, which they check to maintain a heart rate of 160–190 beats per minute for 25-minute stretches at a time throughout the week. When the experimental class started in the fall of 2004, it included about a dozen students who were targeted for extra help on the basis of low reading test scores and teacher recommendations. Reading teachers were also recruited to infuse a bit of literacy instruction into some of the activities. For example, one game calls for students to race around on scooters to match words with their definitions, which are written on pieces of paper on the floor, said Paul Zientarski, the school's instructional coordinator for physical education and health. After their early morning exercise session, the students joined other struggling readers and writers in a special literacy class designed to give them extra academic help in those areas.

At the end of one semester, Naperville educators found, students who took part in the early morning exercise program right before the literacy class earned higher scores than students who had exercised more than two hours before the class or who hadn't exercised at all. Naperville educators tried the same approach the following school year with an introductory algebra class and found that students who both exercised and took a special math class increased their scores on a standardized algebra test by 20.4 percent. The gain for students in the control group was 3.87 percent, according to Zientarski. That finding led guidance counselors to recommend that all students schedule their toughest academic classes right after physical education (Dibble, 2008).

Does advanced placement really work? Some advocates for poor and minority students say that educators should make a concerted effort to reach those students, providing counseling and additional support to encourage their enrollment in rigorous classes (Viadero, 2002). A news story (Welsh, 2006) contrasted two northern Virginia schools, Wakefield High School and T. C. Williams High School, just two miles away from each other. T. C. Williams's student body is about 42 percent black, 24 percent Hispanic, and 27 percent white (plus 7 percent other), whereas Wakefield's is about 29 percent black, 44 percent Hispanic, and 17 percent white (plus 10 percent other). Forty percent of T. C. Williams students and 50 percent of Wakefield students are eligible for free or reduced-price lunch. At the time of the story, the participation rate in AP classes at Wakefield was 36 percent higher than that at T. C. Williams, yet Wakefield's passing rate on AP exams was 51 percent versus T. C. Williams's rate of 39 percent. In other words, rigorous high school courses can actually mitigate the effects of low socioeconomic status.

Southwest High School, a successful comprehensive high school located south of San Diego, promotes rigorous college preparation for all of its students and uses the AVID model as the foundation for its reform efforts. Eighty-four percent of the school's 2,474 students are Hispanic, and 32 percent are designated limited-English-proficient. The AVID program is implemented as an integral part of the school day, and more than 40 percent of the faculty has been trained in the AVID approach. The number of students taking advanced placement tests has increased from 290 to 920 over a four-year period, with about 350 earning passing scores. Ninety percent of the AVID students at Southwest go on to college, almost all of them to four-year colleges.

Action Steps

Implement a strong arts program. This fact cannot be emphasized enough: arts build the student brain's academic operating system. Arts can and should be integrated into all subject areas. At the elementary level, make arts mandatory for at least 30 minutes a day, three to five days a week. Ensure that skill-building classes are taught by a qualified arts teacher. Provide opportunities at the secondary level for music arts (learning musical instruments, singing), visual arts (drawing, painting, graphics, mapping), and kinetic arts (dance, theater).

Step up the activity. Ensure that every single student in your school participates in physical activity a minimum of 30 minutes a day, five days a week. This ought to be nonnegotiable (with exceptions for illness, inclement weather, or serious disabilities).

- Use recess or physical education to engage kids who bully, sit around doing nothing, or dislike the activities offered.
- At every level, get kids who struggle with reading and math into sensory motor labs to engage in sequencing, attentional, and processing tasks that build cognitive capacity.
- Make recess or physical education classes mandatory, not optional or dependent on the time available.
- Offer a variety of choices of gross motor activities to engage in.

Implement an advanced placement curriculum. Once physical activity and the arts have made the brain "fitter," it must then be challenged by higher-level courses. Although conventional wisdom has schools "dumbing down" their curricula to retain high-risk students, a study by Lee and Burkam (2003) revealed that schools that combined rigorous curricula with learner-centered approaches fared much better than did less academically demanding schools or those with negative or uninteresting teaching styles. Students who are challenged with rigorous coursework will step up to the challenge. In fact, a surprisingly large number of kids say that school is not challenging enough (Yazzie-Mintz, 2007). Investigate the possibility of implementing a wider advanced placement curriculum at your school while providing simultaneous support to enhance students' study, memory, and reading skills. Get tutoring for every kid who needs it at no cost. Many secondary schools partner with a local community or university, and undergraduate students often offer tutoring for extra credit or community service. The greater the complexity and difficulty of the curriculum, the greater the need for learning-to-learn skills.

Giving at-risk students a more challenging curriculum may seem questionable on the surface, but the dramatic results of AVID programs throughout the United States put any questions to rest. Instill in kids the belief that this curriculum is doable, that they can excel at it, and that the staff will provide the support needed for success.

Retooling of the Operating System

The enrichment process is not magic. To process new information, students must first develop skills to learn and think in new ways. Although studying the arts, participating in athletics, and taking AP courses may initially seem to be luxuries, especially in at-risk schools, their positive impact on the brain and learning is undeniable. In fact, these "luxuries" may be crucial to student success *especially* at high-risk schools because they provide students with the memory capacity to juggle multiple functions and retrieve others, speed of operations to prevent multiple tasks from bogging down the brain, the capacity to sequence, the ability to focus over time, and a positive attitude. Without these capacities, your students have little chance of succeeding.

In Chapter 3, I discussed the importance of building students' academic operating systems. The better students' operating systems are, the better they'll be able to handle the complex and rigorous challenges that school and life throw at them. The acronym *CHAMPS* stands for the following essential subskills in your students' operating systems:

- **C**hampion's Mind-Set. Students with a champion's mind-set demonstrate an attitude of success and are confident that they can change and learn new behaviors. You can build this skill through modeling and by discussing biographies of relatable successful people and instilling optimism in students.
- **H**opeful Effort. Students who demonstrate hopeful effort have the emotional long-term drive to achieve and the ability to delay gratification. You can build this skill by listening to and encouraging students' hopes and dreams and by teaching goal-setting and study skills.
- **A**ttentional Skills. Students with strong attentional skills possess the ability to stay focused for detailed learning, to shift when needed, and to resist making impulsive decisions. You can build this skill through project-based learning, inquiry, music training, and drama and theater arts.
- **M**emory. Students with good short-term and working memory have high visual and verbal capacity. You can build this skill through in-depth projects, music, and drama.

- Processing Skills. Students with strong processing skills are able to manipulate and manage visual, auditory, and tactile sensory input. You can build this skill through such varied activities as music, cooking, writing, visual arts, critical thinking, and sports.
- Sequencing Skills. Students with strong sequencing skills are organized and able to apply strategies and prioritize tasks and items. You can build this skill through such activities as music, cooking, projects, sports, and math.

Theory and Research

Low-performing schools may recognize that their students underperform, but they aren't teaching the kids how to improve. Retooling students' operating systems means giving them "upgrades" in memory, attention, processing speed, and sequencing skills (Shaywitz et al., 1998), as well as in perceptual-motor skills, auditory processing, volition, and problem-solving skills (Gaab, Gabrieli, Deutsch, Tallal, & Temple, 2007).

Although No Child Left Behind provides that students in schools that continually fail to make adequate yearly progress can receive supplemental educational services, only 20 percent of eligible students are receiving these services, partly because of a lack of quality programs (Burch, Steinberg, & Donovan, 2007). Nonetheless, one-to-one tutoring (Farkas, 1998) and certain computer-based models (Gaab et al., 2007), both of which customize learning to match the precise needs of the student, have been shown to be effective. For example, computer reading programs like Fast ForWord have shown strong gains in as little as 12 weeks (Temple et al., 2003).

Because school time is often booked up with requirements, it may be necessary to create skill-building programs outside school to get the job done. One program aimed at enhancing the educational performance of economically disadvantaged early adolescents who live in public housing had students participate in discussions with adults, engage in writing activities and leisure reading, complete their homework, help others, and play games using cognitive skills. Follow-up data collected after two-and-one-half years revealed uniformly positive outcomes for program youth on measures of reading, verbal skills, writing, and tutoring. Overall grade averages and school attendance in reading, spelling, history, science, and social studies were higher for program youth than for comparison and control youth. The results of programs like these support the value of supplemental skill building in nonschool settings for at-risk youths (Schinke et al., 2000).

Although many real-life situations can help build students' academic operating systems, children raised in poverty are far less likely to be exposed to the enriching experiences that build the *CHAMPS* skill sets. For example, low-SES children are less likely than their well-off peers are to participate in activities that build attentional skills, such as games, sports, arts, and computer-based skill building. Yet attention is the building block for all higher-level cognition (Posner, 2008). One of the fastest ways to make gains is to get students in quality programs that lay the foundation of core skills that will enable rapid gains elsewhere. For example, effort and emotional IQ are teachable traits that enable even low-IQ students to succeed (Mehrabian, 2002). If you want kids to improve fast and dramatically, skill building is among the best things you can do. You'll find little disagreement among educators on the value of skill building; the challenge is in the execution of this concept.

High-Poverty Schools Making It Happen

Every successful school intervention for low-SES kids features some variation on the theme of rebuilding students' academic operating systems. These programs improve students' reading and writing skills, engage them in physical education and the arts, and teach crucial life skills. They are considered standard at schools teaching students with special needs. An effective approach developed by Michael Giangreco (Giangreco, Cloninger, & Iverson, 1998) called COACH (Choosing Outcomes and Accommodations for Children) assesses what the student doesn't know, solicits the student's family's outlook on priorities, and establishes how to teach the identified skills in inclusive environments. The student's IEP team plans and conducts alternative assessments, which help identify areas that need to be shored up. The COACH program

- Identifies family-centered priorities.
- Describes additional learning outcomes.

- Outlines general supports to be provided for the student.
- Translates priorities into IEP goals and objectives.
- Summarizes the educational program as a Program-at-a-Glance.
- Organizes the planning team to implement the program.
- Coordinates participation in general education classes.
- Individualizes lesson plans to facilitate learning.
- Evaluates the impact of educational experiences.

Typically, schools use COACH to identify IEP goals and to document a student's present level of functioning in the selected goals. The planning activities conducted using COACH are then documented in the IEP. Instead of bemoaning underperformance, teachers diagnose the problems and prescribe a specific course of action that provides students with the supplemental help they need to reinforce their basic skills. Farkas and Durham (2007) have concluded that when skill building is poorly executed, results go down. But skill-building programs can work effectively when they match student needs, provide tutoring in smaller groups, are accessible to all students, and require regular student attendance.

A number of schools have incorporated some or all of these components to turn around generally low performance among students. Ira Harbison Elementary in National City, California, a diverse community 12 miles from the United States–Mexico border, has shown impressive increases in student achievement. Sixty percent of the school's students are Hispanic, 45 percent are English language learners (ELLs), and 100 percent are eligible for free or reduced-price lunch. The school also has a 17 percent student mobility rate. In 2002, only 4 percent of ELLs and 28 percent of students overall received a rating of Proficient or higher on the 6th grade reading test, and only 16 percent of ELLs and 40 percent of students overall received a rating of Proficient or higher on the math test. Four years later, 23 percent of ELLs and 45 percent of students overall received a rating of Proficient or higher on the reading test, and 38 percent of ELLs and 49 percent of students overall received a rating of Proficient or higher on the math test. What changed? The school leadership focused on massive upgrades in students' academic operating systems—in particular, their sequencing, processing, and attentional skills. First through 3rd graders now receive three hours of daily targeted literacy instruction, while 4th–6th graders receive two hours, supplemented by additional support and instruction for ELLs.

At high-achieving Sampit Elementary School in Georgetown, South Carolina, the 5th grade assessment data from 2005 indicated that 93 percent of students received a rating of Basic or higher in English language arts, and 88 percent received the same rating in math. Sampit has a strong school-wide focus on reading, requiring students to participate in the 100 Book Challenge sponsored by Harcourt Trophy and American Reading Company, which provide new books to the school several times a year. Sampit also participates in the Accelerated Reader program, and teachers work with individual students to ensure that all students are reading materials at the appropriate levels.

Action Steps

Use a comprehensive 360-degree assessment. Consult the data you've been gathering to determine your students' strengths and weaknesses. Now use a new "lens" to look for student strengths by asking yourself how students are doing on the six *CHAMPS* factors.

Develop and implement a targeted plan. You may be able to use existing programs to rebuild students' operating systems, but the protocol may need to change. To maximize the rate and quality of change, students need consistent, coherent, sustained support in skill building. Implement your programs three to five days a week, allotting 30–90 minutes per day. Ensure the students buy into the program and build in real, just-in-time feedback.

Enrich students' operating systems. Again, use the *CHAMPS* factors to guide you:

- Champion's Mind-Set. Use affirmations, help students with goal setting, tell them about research that says brains can change, and incorporate daily celebrations of learning.
- Hopeful Effort. Use hopeful expressions, build strong relationships, share success stories from positive role models, share strategies to help students meet their goals, celebrate small successes, and provide students with mentors.

- Attentional Skills. Focus on high-interest content to engage students in reading, arts, or games. Teach students to play chess, or have them build something small and detailed.
- Memory. Teach content in small chunks or through a conceptual organizer like a mind map, provide students with memory aids and encoding tools, encourage kinetic activity, and have students practice musical instruments or play chess.
- Processing Skills. Use specialized software like Fast ForWord, have students practice musical instruments or play chess, and use think-out-loud strategies to walk students through critical thinking processes.
- Sequencing Skills. Engage students in project-based learning, have them build or assemble something, ask them to teach a process to their classmates, have them practice musical instruments, and have them play physical games (hopscotch, activities in sensory motor labs) and board games (chess, checkers).

Monitor results and modify skill-building activities as needed. Good intentions aren't enough. Stay on top of your skill-building efforts. Ensure that kids buy in to the process and understand the activities' purposes and objectives well. Be sure to give them constructive, helpful feedback, negative as well as positive. Expect to see results in 4 to 16 weeks, depending on the complexity of the program and its goals.

Skill building can have a strong impact, but only when you maintain your focus on what's truly important and what actually works. Sloppy, haphazard, nontargeted, or large-group instruction will not build specific subskills. If you want to help your low-SES students to succeed, you need to identify their weaknesses in basic skill areas and upgrade their academic operating systems. Only then will they be able to take advantage of the engaging, enriched learning opportunities you have to offer them.

Engaging Instruction

Kids raised in poverty are often victims of inattention in their own homes and, consequently, have poor social skills. How can you reverse the effects of years of neglect and persuade them that school can be personally productive and meaningful? The best way is to engage them in instruction that includes them and their interests in the process.

Theory and Research

In recent years, researchers have formed a strong consensus on the importance of engaged learning. In general, classrooms are not very engaging. The largest annual survey on engagement is conducted by the University of Indiana, which asks an extraordinary sample size of 81,000 kids about their school experiences. Its results are consistently depressing: almost one-half of all secondary students are bored every day, and one out of every six high school students is bored in every single class (Yazzie-Mintz, 2007). If you're looking to make some changes in kids' everyday experiences, this is a great place to start.

Many teachers would rank keeping classroom discipline as one of their top challenges, so much so that there are countless discipline programs on the market for teachers to follow. Not surprisingly, the percentage of 8th grade teachers who reported spending more than one-fifth of their time on classroom discipline increased sharply from 12 percent in low-poverty schools to more than 21 percent in schools whose student populations are more than 40 percent low-SES (Lippman, Burns, & McArthur, 1996). This means that in poor schools, a significant percentage of teachers are frittering away more than one-fifth of their precious hours on power and control struggles. In a school year with 1,000 teaching hours, that's 200 hours—*five work weeks*—spent on behavior corrections! No wonder so many kids from poverty struggle. You don't have time for that. Change your mind-set and start thinking how you can engage their minds and emotions. Engaged kids stay out of trouble; bored kids get into mischief.

Generally speaking, engaging instruction is any strategy that gets students to participate emotionally, cognitively, or behaviorally. Engagement happens when you as an instructional leader stimulate, motivate, and activate. Engagement can result from fun games, intellectual challenges, social interactions, and your own enthusiasm. This process has been well explored, and everyone (e.g., Jensen, 2003; Marzano, 2007; Reeve, 2006) has a different way of understanding, describing, and prescribing engagement. Often, what high school students enjoy most is what they get to do least: engage in discussions and debates, the arts, group projects, and drama (see Figures 5.1 and 5.2).

Although the everyday experiences of elementary kids are typically far more engaging than those of secondary students, there are still concerns. The NICHD Study of Early Child Care and Youth Development was conducted over the course of three years in more than 2,500 1st, 3rd, and 5th grade classrooms and based on live observations of more than 1,000 children around the United States. Pianta, Belsky, Houts, and Morrison (2007) discovered that 5th graders spend 93 percent of their time sitting and working alone (see Figure 5.3)!

Here, according to Jones, Valdez, Nowakowski, and Rasmussen (1994), are the principal indicators of student engagement:

- Students volunteer for class assignments, to complete chores, or simply to answer questions.
- Students do things the first time they are asked and do not have to be nagged.

5.1   What Do Students Enjoy Most?

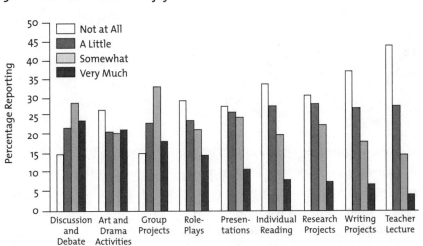

Source: Adapted from *Voices of Students on Engagement: A Report on the 2006 High School Survey of Student Engagement,* by E. Yazzie-Mintz, 2007, Bloomington, IN: Center for Evaluation and Education Policy, Indiana University.

5.2 How Often Are Students Bored?

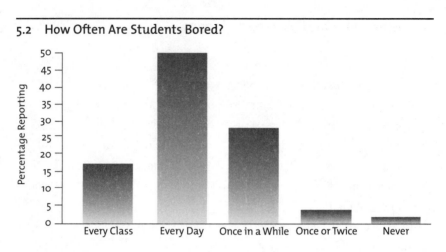

This bar graph depicts student responses to the question "Have you ever been bored in high school?"

Source: Adapted from *Voices of Students on Engagement: A Report on the 2006 High School Survey of Student Engagement,* by E. Yazzie-Mintz, 2007, Bloomington, IN: Center for Evaluation and Education Policy, Indiana University.

- Students participate in after-school activities, such as clubs, sports, or social events.
- In cooperative groups, students listen actively, ask questions, and make contributions.
- Students actively participate in their own learning, get involved in making decisions in the course of their study, conduct vigorous research, think of ideas for projects, and use technology to make discoveries based on their choices.

Student engagement speaks volumes about teachers and schools' academic climate. Engagement happens when students are choosing to attend, participate, and learn. Every one of the schools I have profiled in this book makes engagement a high priority, but let's take a closer look at a few that epitomize the principles and benefits of engaged learning.

High-Poverty Schools Making It Happen

In January 2003, Curtis Middle School in San Bernardino, California, narrowly escaped the threat of being closed down. More recently, the school

5.3 Distribution of Class Time for 5th Graders

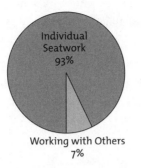

Source: Adapted from "Teaching: Opportunities to Learn in America's Elementary Classrooms," by R. C. Pianta, J. Belsky, R. Houts, and F. Morrison, 2007, *Science, 315*(5820), pp. 1795–1796.

has satisfied 13 of 25 adequate yearly progress criteria. Currently, 97 per-cent of the school's students are eligible for free or reduced-price lunch. Curtis attributes its transformation to having teachers become leaders on the campus. The teachers implemented a structured professional learning community to find ways to increase student motivation and engagement schoolwide. They began a five-month cycle of research, observation, collabo-ration, implementation, and assessment during a two-hour weekly block of professional development time. During the first month, teachers researched a strategy; the next month, the leader teachers demonstrated the strategy in lessons attended by the other teachers. Next, teachers met to discuss their insights, any questions they still had, and ways to implement the strategy in their own classes. Teachers then implemented the strategy as administra-tors gathered informal data on the implementation. Finally, teachers met to examine student work and other measures and conducted self-assessments to find ways to improve their use of the strategy. This professional develop-ment led to a culture of trust and collaboration among the teachers and a family environment throughout the school (Atkins & Rossi, 2007), leading to fewer discipline problems and increased student engagement.

The design of San Diego's High Tech High (HTH), an independent public charter school designed to serve 600 students in grades 7–12, is based on three key principles: personalization, adult world connection, and common intellectual mission. The school was conceived by a group of local high-technology business leaders and educators to address the high-tech industry's problems of finding qualified people to fill the growing number of job opportunities in the area. In this case, technology is used as the hook to increase engagement. Innovative features include performance-based assessment, daily shared planning time for staff, state-of-the-art technical facilities for project-based learning, internships for all students, and close links to the high-tech workplace.

HTH is a performance-based school: every student creates a digital portfolio that provides a comprehensive look at his or her work and learning. Each digital portfolio includes a personal statement, a résumé, work samples, and information about projects and internships. The digital portfolio is mapped to the traditional high school transcript to ensure that HTH's students can demonstrate their learning and educational achievements in ways that fit the standard measurements of achievement used by the state and by colleges and universities. Student projects include building robots, a hovercraft, and a submarine and producing a video on Japanese internment camps during World War II. Art is also integrated into all aspects of the curriculum and appears throughout the school.

HTH's emphasis on project-based learning helps students develop a personal connection to their work. Students explore their individual interests and passions and collaborate with adults on work whose meaning goes beyond that of a graded course. Every junior or senior completes at least one term-long internship outside the school. All of HTH's graduates have gone on to college. The school's API Statewide Rank score is 10, meaning the school's Academic Performance Index fell into the top 10 percent in California. HTH also has the highest test scores in the state for Latino students and disadvantaged youth.

In Long Beach, California, there is a high-minority school that never has issues with engagement. Founding director Marvin Smith has developed a school that is focused on providing opportunities rarely made available to low-SES kids. Like many schools that succeed with kids raised in poverty, the Micro-Enterprise Charter Academy has a rigorous curriculum of academic preparation and college readiness. In fact, all students participate in college-preparatory coursework that explicitly teaches academic, social, and financial strategies for obtaining a college education. But the school's genius lies in how it achieves this. Smith gives students the tools to collapse the digital divide between different socioeconomic classes, and all students apply technological solutions (e.g., multimedia presentations, spreadsheet applications, Web design, and project management tools) to academic and real-world situations. They all engage in ongoing entrepreneurship projects, in which students work on community projects and think of potential future career opportunities and business ideas, and students design and implement micro-enterprises with explicitly taught leadership skills. Graduation rates are through the roof, and kids love coming to school.

Action Steps

One of the most powerful ways to engage students is to let them take charge of their own learning. Students know their seats, their working partners, and where the learning supplies are located. They are self-regulated and come up with learning goals and problems that are meaningful to them. They manage their own time and use rubrics or checklists to manage the quality of their work. These students are more likely to find passion, excitement, and pleasure in learning. Teachers serve as coaches or facilitators, guiding students to the desired goals. Students participate in real-life activities through collaboration, exploration, and discovery with peers. Students do not walk into your class pre-assembled this way. They need encouragement, training, coaching, and support.

Find, recruit, and train the best staff you can find. To start this process, strike up a conversation at conferences with the best to discover how to attract strong teachers to your school. Ask some of the best teachers in your district what it would take to get them to teach in one of the district's most challenging schools. Some will tell you they can't handle the commute, others would need a change in colleagues, and some may even say the school needs painting. At least decide if you can change anything to attract the best.

Gather information from students. Remember, we get kids for only 30 hours a week, and we have to be dead-on to transform their lives. Administer a 10-question survey that asks students how often they feel excited, supported, and actively engaged in the learning process. If your school is not consistently engaging, you're losing your kids. Find out how often kids are bored; many staff members will need empirical evidence before they can accept that the kids they are teaching are not compelled to even participate.

Communicate the evidence and make a plan. Once you have the data, share them with the staff in a nonthreatening way. Do not say "This is how boring you are," but "This is what our kids say." The survey is just feedback, not a crucifixion. Then, consult available resources, brainstorm as a group, or solicit ideas from the most engaging teachers to develop a list of engagement strategies for each teacher to use.

Add a strategy each week and monitor progress. Engaging students means more than increasing social interactions or using more technology. In fact, highly engaging teachers tend to use a host of strategies that keep students involved nonstop in the learning process (Jensen, 2003). Most teachers can succeed if they have just one new strategy to apply each week. Let them try something out, get comfortable with it, tweak it, and make it automatic. The goal is to manage students' emotional states to make them receptive to learning as much of the time as possible. It can be done, and here's how to do it:

- Switch up social groups. Mix up the class time so that kids are only in one social grouping for 10–20 minutes at a time. Use study buddies, assigned teams, whole-class activities, or temporary ad hoc partnerships.
- Incorporate movement through learning stations, class switching, and assemblies. Class switching allows teachers who are strong in physical activities to take on another teacher's kids for a short time both to show the other teacher how to incorporate movement and to give the kids a high-energy physical break. Assemblies can incorporate energizing fan rituals like dancing or the wave.
- Ask more compelling questions; avoid unanswerable rhetorical questions. Include your entire class in your questions: instead of asking "Who saw [XYZ movie] last weekend?" ask "How many of you have seen or experienced *this* in your life?" This way, you end up including those who didn't see the movie but who share a common experience featured in the movie.
- Appreciate and acknowledge every response. When you make a habit of thanking students for putting themselves out there, you'll see more hands up in the air. Don't feel the need to evaluate everything they say.

Don't say "Well, that's not entirely true." Instead, say "Thanks for jumping in. Let's grab a few more comments, then we'll debrief them all to figure out what we have here."

• Use energizers, games, drama, simulations, and other demonstration strategies.

• Keep the content alive with call-backs, hand raisers, stretching, and unfinished sentences and review questions.

• Be passionate about what you teach so that students are drawn into the emotional drama of the content.

It can be challenging to find ways to encourage disadvantaged students to embrace classrooms and a school system that historically have worked against them, but these students can still be positively surprised by what happens in their classrooms. Interaction with the physical world and with other people enables students to discover concepts and apply skills. By integrating what they have learned, students themselves become producers of knowledge, capable of making significant contributions to the world's knowledge base. What they have learned and how they learned it not only are important in their own right but also validate students' self-worth.

One important caveat: there are limits to the sheer quantity of content that students of any socioeconomic status can take in during a class period or day. Our brains allow for unlimited "priming effect" exposure, meaning we can get a superficial exposure to names, people, and events over time that gives us a notion about the content. But to process content and build in-depth understandings, students need time. Our brains may have limited vocabulary or prior knowledge. They have limited working memory and need time to recycle proteins and glucose and to consolidate new learning at the synapse and create connections. In short, engaging classes build in processing time. There are hundreds of strategies than can help students process each body of content better (Jensen & Nickelsen, 2008), but most important is this ratio: never use more than 50 percent of instructional time to deliver new content. If you give students at least half the time to process the content, they will understand and remember it longer. You can teach faster, but students will just forget faster (Alvarez & Cavanagh, 2004; Izawa, 2000; Klingberg, 2000; Todd & Marois, 2004; Wood, 2002).

The Extras

The power of the strategies discussed in this chapter is that although they are designed to build success with low-SES students, they will work well with students of all income levels. There is no need to reserve these classroom strategies for certain groups of students. They just happen to be of greater value to schools working with kids from poverty. For example, I can give vitamin supplements to 1,000 kids. For those who eat well, exercise, and manage their stress, the supplements may be of less value. But for those who don't follow that healthy routine, supplements may provide an extra boost that makes all the difference. Similarly, in the classroom, some of these strategies may not be a big deal to every single student. But to some, they make all the difference. Never, ever give up those "extras."

6

Instructional Light and Magic

Veteran teacher Chris Hawkins is starting to feel as though change just might happen for him. He feels willing to make a renewed commitment to his profession, his students, and himself. Ask him and he'll tell you that he's now "on board." His current biggest challenge is to work out the many new strategies he's learned and apply them in his history class; he's been a "stand and deliver" teacher for so long. But Mr. Hawkins now knows that if he wants things to change, *he* has to change. Now he's asking for some help. He has read books on improving his teaching, so he knows what to do; he just doesn't understand exactly how and when to do it. He's thinking about retirement differently these days. He's thinking, "I want to get this figured out fast. Retirement is coming up way too quickly."

A Day in the Life of Mr. Hawkins's Classroom

The data are pretty convincing; regardless of overall school policies, teachers' daily value is substantial (Nye, Konstantopoulos, & Hedges, 2004). Even if your school has only one outstanding teacher, that teacher can still act as a role model. The principal can substitute for teachers in turn while they leave their classes to observe the exemplary teacher in practice. Sometimes you've got to see it to believe it.

This chapter pulls together the book's core ideas by following Mr. Hawkins through a typical Monday. This may help you better visualize how you can apply the practices in your own classroom. You may notice that not every strategy is mentioned here. That wasn't an accident; it's just not productive to list every single classroom minute of the day and every single thing teachers should do. Presumably, teachers are already aware of many of these things. Here, I focus on the factors that matter most, the better to highlight the differences that will reshape the brains and enrich the lives of your kids.

The phrase "instructional light and magic" refers to your ability to shine a spotlight on what matters most. Then get ready for the magic, because it will happen.

Before Class

Collecting data. Mr. Hawkins, our history teacher, has 32 students: 15 boys and 17 girls. Two are pregnant, and 5 are being raised by caregivers rather than parents. Mr. Hawkins has surveyed his class and learned that 8 students really like NBA basketball, 22 are into music, and the majority are dominantly kinesthetic learners. He has also found out that 80 percent of his class earned low scores in descriptive writing and reading comprehension.

Planning. Mr. Hawkins thinks about particular students who need extra help. He has made plans well ahead of time to ensure their success. He'll use preteaching, priming, and a quick buddy review. He walks through his lesson in advance, asking himself, "How will I engage students? How will I make the content come alive? How will I ensure that it's memorable?" He has prepared his iPod with special themed playlists: class openings, reflection music, energizing tunes, seatwork soundtrack, special effects, and closing-the-class music.

Making personal preparations. Mr. Hawkins hydrates before class, eats an energy bar, and listens to his favorite music to get ready for his students' arrival. He knows that when he's in a positive state, his students notice and have a better class experience.

Creating a positive physical environment. Mr. Hawkins has some limitations in terms of his classroom environment, so he focuses on what matters most: ensuring sufficient ventilation, acoustics, and lighting and posting useful content on his walls, including new vocabulary words, how-to-write models, charts of how the different class teams are doing, key upcoming ideas, and positive affirmations. What he cannot influence, he lets go of. Upbeat, positive music plays as students arrive. Today, his iPod is playing

"Ain't No Stopping Us," "You Can Make It If You Try," "I'm into Something Good," and "You Are My Number One."

First 10 Minutes of Class Time

Mr. Hawkins now knows more about what kids need than he ever did before, including strong relationships, hope, engagement, success, and respect. He developed the following beginning-of-class six-step sequence to fulfill those needs.

Building relationships. Each Monday morning, Mr. Hawkins greets every student at the door with a positive affirmation ("Good morning, Jasmine! It's good to see you—get ready for a great week"). He doesn't do this every other day of the week, but Monday is special; his personal greetings get the week off to a good start.

Getting started. Mr. Hawkins plays the "class song" that his students chose from a selection of positive songs he offered. He times the song so that even after the bell rings, the kids get about one minute of pre-class social time. This extra minute allows students to catch up with one another and gives Mr. Hawkins an opportunity to see what's going on in his kids' lives. For example, there may have been an eviction, an illness, a parent who left, or even a death in the neighborhood. Mr. Hawkins uses this student social time to listen in or simply watch body language. When the song ends, class starts.

Boosting social status. To support social status and make sure every student feels included, Mr. Hawkins has divided his class into teams. Students start class by sitting with their "home" teams. They know their teams lose points if they are not all seated by the time the class song ends. The points give teams "bragging rights," but no other privileges. Each team has a name, a cheer, a leader, and a weekly performance chart posted on the wall. The role of team leader is rotated so that every student gets a chance to lead at some point during the school year. Each week, students engage in team-building activities as well as working on projects.

Taking care of administrative tasks. All the class business (attendance, announcements, and so on) is conducted by team leaders within the first 30–60 seconds of class. The team leaders give the attendance to Mr. Hawkins, and the team leader whose turn it is reads the daily announcements to the class. Mr. Hawkins uses this time to appreciate one thing about that student ("I liked the volume of your voice") and make one suggestion ("Look out at all your classmates first before speaking"). This process teaches every student a bit of poise and a few social skills over the semester.

Connecting with real life. Every Monday, Mr. Hawkins tells the class something about his weekend. This true story might be funny, sad, dramatic, petty, or intriguing. During this one-to-two-minute period, students connect personally with Mr. Hawkins. He knows that for many kids, a stable, caring adult is important in their lives. Sometimes his stories are about the everyday problems he encounters, like registering a car, a silly disagreement he had with his wife, or getting his online bank account set up. Once he brings up a problem, Mr. Hawkins will often turn it over to the teams to solve, asking them, "What would you do if you were me? How would you get out of this jam if you were dealt this card in life?" This simple activity fosters students' problem-solving skills and teaches them how to play the "cards" they are dealt in life. He encourages kids to become participants in life, not spectators.

Jump-starting the brain. At the beginning of each class, Mr. Hawkins runs through a quick review using one of seven or eight strategies in his repertoire; each takes no more than five minutes, requires no planning, and uses minimal materials. Today's review strategy is a team fill-in activity. Mr. Hawkins uses a PowerPoint presentation to show a graphic organizer of the previous class's key concepts. About 12 words of the 25–30 total words are missing on the mind map. Every team gets three minutes to figure out what content belongs and where it goes. Mr. Hawkins spurs a little competitive spirit, but he keeps it in good fun. When the three-minute time limit is up, he reviews the results and corrects errors. This activity gives students a review of the last class, and it gives Mr. Hawkins an idea of where he needs to focus.

Core Class Time

Making it relevant. After you've gotten students' attention comes the tricky part of engaging students' interest. Making the topic relevant and creating buy-in activates neuronal assemblies, also known as networks, in particular ways that influence states. "Today, you'll learn how an entire presidential election was stolen from a candidate, right in front of everyone's eyes.

And it was all legal. How do you think they pulled that off? Working in your teams, come up with your best guess." After the teams meet, Mr. Hawkins has a student list each team's predictions on a whiteboard.

Building hope. Mr. Hawkins makes sure to incorporate hope building as he teaches. He keeps a stack of 3 × 5 cards with simple strategies to use. In time, the process will become automatic and he'll include them in the lesson without thinking. Today, he's remembering to ask at least two kids about their dreams and to affirm them with confidence. It feels funny to do that, he admits, but it's a start. He never used to do anything close to it. As a kid, he had always had hope: trying to build it in others seems artificial. But he knows it's essential.

Building the operating system. Mr. Hawkins is conscious of the importance of building crucial learning skills as he teaches. As with hope building, he keeps a stack of 3 × 5 cards listing simple strategies that will eventually become second nature. For now, he diligently rotates his strategies: "Today, I'm going to show you a cool way to help you remember what you learn, so you'll be able to spend less time studying but know things even better." He goes on to show his students how to use mind maps to take much better notes and to sequence and process them for better retention.

Getting physical. Mr. Hawkins knows his students don't perceive how much control they have over their feelings. Because negative states of worry, disengagement, and distress all contribute to lower cognitive performance, and positive emotional states help students learn more, managing emotional states has become a challenging "sideline" task. Working memory needs dopamine for optimal functioning, and Mr. Hawkins knows that a good way to boost it is to engage in fun physical activities. The fringe benefit is a boost in heart rate, circulation to the brain, and production of other "uppers" for the brain, like adrenaline. Every 12 to 15 minutes, Mr. Hawkins ensures that students are up, out of their seats, and doing something physical. Some of his favorites have students

- "Jigsaw" new learning by spreading out to join other teams, then returning and sharing what they learned.
- Stand up, touch three walls, find a partner, and engage in the think-pair-share strategy.

- Stand and select one team member to lead the rest of the team in 30 seconds of a dance step or other energizer.
- Stand up and form a new group with non–team members and play kinesthetic math games.
- Stand in the middle of the room and vote on matters of opinion with their bodies. For example, if they agree with a given statement, they go to the left side of the room; if they disagree, they go to the right side.
- Touch 12 chairs and find a partner. Each partner takes a side in a debate and gets 30 seconds to make a case for his or her assigned point of view. Then they switch sides and debate the topic again.

Mr. Hawkins has learned some of the secrets to conducting successful classroom activities. For example, he always gives just one direction at a time, which manages the actions better. He is familiar with the recent research (Gobet & Clarkson, 2004) suggesting that our working memory maxes out at two items. And although many teachers complain that once you get kids revved up, it's hard to calm them down, Mr. Hawkins understands the value of calming activities. He often leads a brief ritual of visualizing or deep breathing to bring his students back to an attentive state of mind.

Framing the content. Mr. Hawkins used to complain that his kids weren't vested enough in the content. Now he knows to use such strategies as *framing,* known in political circles as putting a spin on things. This powerful strategy creates an intentional bias toward what follows so that students are more likely to "buy into" the content. You can frame a word, an activity, an assignment, or a whole class. Framing is the set-up for a story, the background for an activity, or anything else that "hooks" the learner mentally. Framing creates an emotional invitation to learn. Today, Mr. Hawkins reads a riveting autobiographical passage that gets students thinking about the lesson. It's about an African American man who was drafted during the Vietnam War but who could not vote in his hometown because of illegal voter registration quirks. This reading springboarded a conversation about prejudice, both at the national level and at school.

Delivering the content. Today, Mr. Hawkins is going the cooperative, or collaborative, learning route. He has broken the unit on post–World War II elections into three essential questions for the week. The questions match up with the standards that students are expected to know. Each team will be responsible for exploring one of the questions. Mr. Hawkins gives each of the teams the questions to explore, the tree-branch hierarchy of the information to learn, key vocabulary words, and meaning-making personal questions about the topic. Before students begin their quest, Mr. Hawkins reviews the information sources (books, the Internet, DVDs, articles, and so on) and tells an emotional war story about the historical period being studied that hooks everyone. When he's finished telling the story, he shares that it was real; it was about his experience in Vietnam. The students begin the assignment. They have 20 minutes to work as a team to decide who will do what and to begin gathering information.

Elaborating and correcting errors. Mr. Hawkins has learned the value of error correction. Positive reinforcement is great for boosting student morale, but the process of making and correcting mistakes is necessary to build not only the academic operating system but also the social operating system (see Figure 6.1). Learning by making mistakes rather than by being lectured at or

---

6.1   Six Crucial Areas of the Social Operating System

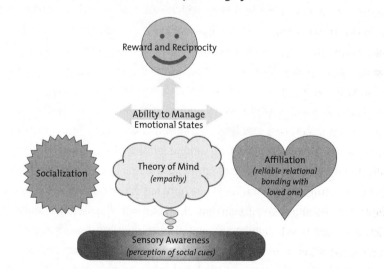

Most students need to strengthen the six social attributes depicted here. These qualities can improve classroom climate and increase students' chances for success in school.

immediately told the correct solution requires a safe environment that provides plenty of chances to make mistakes and correct errors. In today's class, it's more information gathering because the elaboration will be happening over the next couple of days. There will be time tomorrow for the digging and processing. Mr. Hawkins also administers a quiz twice a week. It's never a surprise, always predictably given on Tuesday and Friday. He knows the research: repeated testing on the same content produces better scores than repetition, studying, or new testing (Karpicke & Roediger, 2008).

Last 10 Minutes of Class Time

Strengthening memory. Near the end of every class, Mr. Hawkins wisely sets aside this time. During this segment, he reviews the content from the last two weeks in an easy-to-recall format, using acronyms, graphic organizers, callbacks, and rhymes. He ensures that every student feels successful before he or she leaves for the day.

Assigning homework. Mr. Hawkins gives out a list of optional short-answer homework questions at the beginning of each unit and allows five minutes at the end of class for doing homework. This is an example of an accommodation that levels the playing field and shows an understanding of the world of poverty. During this time, he provides individual help and collects homework from those who are done. No student is penalized for not doing homework; it just helps Mr. Hawkins get a better understanding of his kids.

Cleaning up. Mr. Hawkins conducts more than a dozen rituals that get class jobs (e.g., cleanup) done in a productive way. For the last two minutes of class, teams know that it's time to get the class back in top shape. Everything needs to be put away, organized, and cleaned up. He plays a wrapping-up song called "Hold On to Your Dreams." The teams move quickly, humming the words. When they finish, each team celebrates with its team cheer, and the energy is high. The goal is always to be cleaned up and ready to go by the last note of the song. During this time, Mr. Hawkins again is building relationships. He knows that he must ramp up his relationship building by enhancing social status, fostering an inclusive environment, mentoring, and being a stable, reliable, supportive adult in students' lives.

Closing the day. During the last minute of class, there's always time for an affirmation to teammates, a cliffhanger story for next time, or a brief visualization of success. Asking kids to visualize success on an upcoming skill or knowledge set is no "New Age" strategy. When done well, mental practice is known not only to make physical changes in the brain but also to improve task performance (Pascual-Leone, Amedi, Fregni, & Merabet, 2005). Mr. Hawkins makes it a point to end the class on a high note.

Enriching Minds, Changing Lives

Critics may say that Mr. Hawkins's class has more fluff than substance. That's exactly what Mr. Hawkins would have said a few short years ago, before he began to understand what kids raised in poverty need. Note that in his class structure, he invests *part* of his allotment of time in managing students' emotional states. When you've got only a few hours a week to counter the effects of years of poverty, you can't waste a minute. Teachers like Mr. Hawkins have learned to provide emotional support while they engage students' interest and build their intellectual skills. Mr. Hawkins's students are excited and motivated and have fewer discipline problems than they used to. Mr. Hawkins likes the changes he is seeing and now refers to his students as "my kids." On their part, kids actually enjoy being in his classes.

Good teaching can mitigate the effects of low socioeconomic status and lack of school resources. Your staff is the key to students' success, and it's time to rethink how they use their time. The quality of your students' education will not exceed the aggregate quality of the teaching staff at your school. Every school staff has to find its own way; there is no magic formula or silver bullet to solve every problem and turn all low-SES kids into high achievers. But we do know that school turnarounds are accomplished by fostering caring relationships that build students' resilience and self-esteem, by setting high academic standards in the belief that all students can learn, and by initiating a focused and collaborative effort among staff members, parents, and the community to engage and challenge students to learn the things they need to learn.

Take a moment and visualize the members of your staff. You'll notice a wide range of interests, skills, political views, backgrounds, and knowledge areas. Now imagine them at sunrise, starting their respective days: they are asking either "How long until retirement?" or "What miracles can I create today?" Which question are *your* teachers asking? Is it time for you and your school to take the plunge? Are you up for the challenge? Breathe easy; you can do it. Join the efforts, sell the vision, make the plans, take action, and join the celebration.

References

Adelman, C. (1999). *Answers in the tool box: Academic intensity, attendance patterns, and bachelor's degree attainment*. Washington, DC: U.S. Department of Education, Office of Educational Research and Improvement.

Ahnert, L., Pinquart, M., & Lamb, M. (2006). Security of children's relationships with nonparental care provider. *Child Development, 77*(3), 664–679.

Almeida, D. M., Neupert, S. D., Banks, S. R., & Serido, J. (2005). Do daily stress processes account for socioeconomic health disparities? *Journal of Gerontology Series B: Psychological Sciences and Social Sciences, 60*(2), 34–39.

Alvarez, G. A., & Cavanagh, P. (2004). The capacity of visual short-term memory is set both by visual information load and by number of objects. *Psychological Science, 15*(2), 106–111.

Angelo, T. A. (1993, April). A "teacher's dozen": Fourteen general, research-based principles for improving higher learning in our classrooms. *AAHE Bulletin, 45*(8), 3–7, 13.

Astone, N. M., Misra, D., & Lynch, C. (2007). The effect of maternal socio-economic status throughout the lifespan on infant birth weight. *Paediatric and Perinatal Epidemiology, 21*(4), 310–318.

Atkins, K., & Rossi, M. (2007). Change from within. *Educational Leadership, 65*(1), 1–5.

Attar, B. K., Guerra, N. G., & Tolan, P. H. (1994). Neighborhood disadvantage, stressful life events, and adjustment in urban elementary-school children. *Journal of Clinical Child Psychology, 23,* 391–400.

Atzaba-Poria, N., Pike, A., & Deater-Deckard, K. (2004). Do risk factors for problem behaviour act in a cumulative manner? An examination of ethnic minority and majority children through an ecological perspective. *Journal of Child Psychology and Psychiatry, 45*(4), 707–718.

Barnett, W. S. (1995). Long-term effects of early childhood care and education on disadvantaged children's cognitive development and school success. *The Future of Children, 5*(3), 25–50.

Barnett, W. S. (1998). Long-term cognitive and academic effects of early childhood education on children in poverty. *Preventive Medicine, 27*(2), 204–207.

Baydar, N., Brooks-Gunn, J., & Furstenberg, F. (1993). Early warning signs of functional illiteracy: Predictors in childhood and adolescence. *Child Development, 64*(3), 815–829.

Bjørnebekk, A., Mathé, A. A., & Brené, S. (2005). The antidepressant effect of running is associated with increased hippocampal cell proliferation. *The International Journal of Neuropsychopharmacology, 8*(3), 357–368.

Blair, C., Granger, D. A., Kivlighan, K. T., Mills-Koonce, R., Willoughby, M., Greenberg, M. T., et al. (2008). Maternal and child contributions to cortisol response to emotional arousal in young children from low-income, rural communities. *Developmental Psychology, 44*(4), 1095–1109.

Bolland, L., Lian, B. E., & Formichella, C. M. (2005). The origins of hopelessness among inner-city African-American adolescents. *American Journal of Community Psychology, 36*(3/4), 293–305.

Bornstein, M. H., Haynes, M. O., & Painter, K. M. (1998). Sources of child vocabulary competence: A multivariate model. *Journal of Child Language, 25*(2), 367–393.

Boston Public Schools. (1998, March 9). *High school restructuring.* Boston: Author.

Bracey, G. W. (2006). Poverty's infernal mechanism. *Principal Leadership, 6*(6), 60.

Bradley, R. H., & Corwyn, R. F. (2002, February). Socioeconomic status and child development. *Annual Review of Psychology, 53,* 371–399.

Bradley, R. H., Corwyn, R. F., Burchinal, M., McAdoo, H. P., & Coll, C. G. (2001). The home environments of children in the United States, Part II: Relations with behavioral development through age thirteen. *Child Development, 72*(6), 1868–1886.

Bradley, R. H., Corwyn, R. F., McAdoo, H. P., & Coll, C. G. (2001). The home environments of children in the United States, Part I: Variations by age, ethnicity, and poverty status. *Child Development, 72*(6), 1844–1867.

Bradley, R. H., Whiteside-Mansell, L., Mundfrom, D. J., Casey, P. H., Kelleher, K. J., & Pope, S. K. (1994). Early indications of resilience and their relation to experiences in the home environments of low birthweight, premature children living in poverty. *Child Development, 65*(2), 346–360.

Bradmetz, J., & Mathy, F. (2006). An estimate of the Flynn effect: Changes in IQ and subtest gains of 10-yr-old French children between 1965 and 1988. *Psychological Reports, 99*(3), 743–746.

Bridgman, A., & Phillips, D. (1998). *New findings on poverty and child health and nutrition: Summary of a research briefing.* Washington, DC: National Academy Press.

Broadman, J. D. (2004). Stress and physical health: The role of neighborhoods as mediating and moderating mechanisms. *Social Science and Medicine, 58*(12), 2473–2483.

Brooks-Gunn, J., Guo, G., & Furstenberg, F. (1993). Who drops out of and who continues beyond high school? *Journal of Research on Adolescence, 3*(3), 271–294.

Brooks-Gunn, J., McCarton, C., Casey, P., McCormick, M., Bauer, C., Bernbaum, J., et al. (1994). Early intervention in low birthweight, premature infants. *Journal of the American Medical Association, 272,* 1257–1262.

Bruel-Jungerman, E., Rampon, C., & Laroche, S. (2007). Adult hippocampal neurogenesis, synaptic plasticity and memory: Facts and hypotheses. *Reviews in the Neurosciences, 18*(2), 93–114.

Burch, P., Steinberg, M., & Donovan, J. (2007). Supplemental educational services and NCLB: Policy assumptions, market practices, emerging issues. *Educational Evaluation and Policy Analysis, 29*(2), 115–133.

Cage, B., & Smith, J. (2000). The effects of chess instruction on mathematics achievement of southern, rural, black, secondary students. *Research in the Schools, 7*(1), 9–26.

Campbell, F. A., Pungello, E. P., Miller-Johnson, S., Burchinal, M., & Ramey, C. T. (2001). The development of cognitive and academic abilities: Growth curves from an early childhood educational experiment. *Developmental Psychology, 37*(2), 231–242.

Campbell, F. A., & Ramey, C. T. (1994, April). Effects of early intervention on intellectual and academic achievement: A follow-up study of children from low-income families. *Child Development, 65,* 684–698.

Capron, C., & Duyme, M. (1989). Assessment of effects of socio-economic status on IQ in a full cross-fostering study. *Nature, 340,* 552–554.

Carraher, T. N., Carraher, D., & Schliemann, A. D. (1985). Mathematics in the streets and in schools. *British Journal of Developmental Psychology, 3,* 21–29.

Carter, S. C. (2000). *No excuses: 21 lessons from high-performing, high-poverty schools.* Washington, DC: Heritage Foundation.

Cartwright, M., Wardle, J., Steggles, N., Simon, A. E., Croker, H., & Jarvis, M. J. (2003). Stress and dietary practices in adolescents. *Health Psychology, 22*(4), 362–369.

Catterall, J. S., Chapleau, R., & Iwanaga, J. (1999). Involvement in the arts and human development: General involvement and intensive involvement in music and theatre arts. In E. B. Fiske (Ed.), *Champions of change: The impact of the arts on learning* (pp. 48–62). Washington, DC: Arts Education Partnership.

Ceci, S. J. (1991). How much does schooling influence general intelligence and its cognitive components? A reassessment of the evidence. *Developmental Psychology, 27*(5), 703–722.

Ceci, S. (2001, July 1). IQ to the test. *Psychology Today.* Retrieved March 17, 2007, from http://psychologytoday.com/articles/pto-20010701-000024.html

Ceci, S. J., & Liker, J. (1986). A day at the races: A study of IQ, expertise, and cognitive complexity. *Journal of Experimental Psychology: General, 115,* 255–266.

Chan, A. S., Ho, Y. C., & Cheung, M. C. (1998). Music training improves verbal memory. *Nature, 396,* 128.

Chasnoff, I. J., Anson, A., Hatcher, R., Stenson, H., Iaukea, K., & Randolph, L. (1998). Prenatal exposure to cocaine and other drugs. Outcome at four to six years. *Annals of the New York Academy of Sciences, 846,* 314–328.

Chaudhari, S., Otiv, M., Chitale, A., Hoge, M., Pandit, A., & Mote, A. (2005). Biology versus environment in low birth weight children. *Indian Pediatrics, 42*(8), 763–770.

Checkley, K. (1995). Multiyear education: Reaping the benefits of "looping." *Education Update, 37*(8), 1, 3, 6.

Chenoweth, K. (2007). *"It's being done": Academic success in unexpected schools.* Cambridge, MA: Harvard Education Press.

Coley, R. (2002). *An uneven start: Indicators of inequality in school readiness.* Princeton, NJ: Educational Testing Service.

Conrad, C. D. (2006). What is the functional significance of chronic stress-induced CA3 dendritic retraction within the hippocampus? *Behavioral and Cognitive Neuroscience Reviews, 5*(1), 41–60.

Constantino, R. (2005). Print environments between high and low socioeconomic status (SES) communities. *Teacher Librarian, 32*(3), 22–25.

Cook, S. C., & Wellman, C. L. (2004). Chronic stress alters dendritic morphology in rat medial prefrontal cortex. *Neurobiology, 60*(2), 236–248.

Cooper, H., Nye, B., Charlton, K., Lindsay, J., & Greathouse, S. (1996). The effects of summer vacation on achievement test scores: A narrative and meta-analytic review. *Review of Educational Research, 66*(3), 227–268.

Coplan, J. D., Andrews, M. W., Rosenblum, L. A., Owens, M. J., Friedman, S., Gorman, J. M., et al. (1996). Persistent elevations of cerebrospinal fluid concentrations of corticotropin-releasing factor in adult nonhuman primates exposed to early-life stressors: Implications for the pathophysiology of mood and anxiety disorders. *Proceedings of the National Academy of Sciences of the United States of America, 93,* 1619–1623.

Cotton, K. (2003). *Principals and student achievement.* Alexandria, VA: ASCD.

Datnow, A., Hubbard, L., & Mehan, H. (2002). *Extending educational reform: From one school to many.* New York: Routledge Falmer.

Davis, O. S., Kovas, Y., Harlaar, N., Busfield, P., McMillan, A., Frances, J., et al. (2008). Generalist genes and the Internet generation: Etiology of learning abilities by web testing at age 10. *Genes, Brain, and Behavior, 7*(4), 455–462.

De Bellis, M. D. (2005). The psychobiology of neglect. *Child Maltreatment, 10*(2), 150–172.

De Bellis, M. D., Keshavan, M. S., Beers, S. R., Hall, J., Frustaci, K., Masalehdan, A., et al. (2001). Sex differences in brain maturation during childhood and adolescence. *Cerebral Cortex, 11*(6), 552–557.

DeGarmo, D. S., Forgatch, M. S., & Martinez, C. R. (1999). Parenting of divorced mothers as a link between social status and boys' academic outcomes: Unpacking the effects of socioeconomic status. *Child Development, 70,* 1231–1245.

Denny, S., Clark, T., Fleming, T., & Wall, M. (2004). Emotional resilience: Risk and protective factors for depression among alternative education students in New Zealand. *American Journal of Orthopsychiatry, 74*(2), 137–149.

Desimone, L. M., Smith, T. M., Hayes, S. A., & Frisvold, D. (2005). Beyond accountability and average mathematics scores: Relating state education policy attributes to cognitive achievement domains. *Educational Measurement: Issues and Practice, 24*(4), 5–18.

Devlin, B., Daniels, M., & Roeder, K. (1997). The heritability of IQ. *Nature, 388*(6641), 468–471.

Dibble, S. (2008, January 22). District 203 provided spark for book: Psychiatrist draws connection between physical activity and learning. *Daily Herald* (Illinois). Retrieved May 3, 2008, from www.johnratey.com/Articles/District203providedspark%20.pdf

Dobrossy, M. D., & Dunnett, S. B. (2004). Environmental enrichment affects striatal graft morphology and functional recovery. *European Journal of Neuroscience, 19*(1), 159–168.

Dodge, K. A., Pettit, G. S., & Bates, J. E. (1994). Socialization mediators of the relation between socioeconomic status and child conduct problems. *Child Development, 65*(2), 649–665.

Draganski, B., Gaser, C., Kempermann, G., Kuhn, H. G., Winkler, J., Büchel, C., et al. (2006). Temporal and spatial dynamics of brain structure changes during extensive learning. *The Journal of Neuroscience, 26*(23), 6314–6317.

Driemeyer, J., Boyke, J., Gaser, C., Büchel, C., & May, A. (2008). Changes in gray matter induced by learning—Revisited. *PLoS ONE, 3*(7), e2669.

DuBois, D. L., & Silverthorn, N. (2004). Do deviant peer associations mediate the contributions of self-esteem to problem behavior during early adolescence? A 2-year longitudinal study. *Journal of Clinical Child and Adolescent Psychology, 33*(2), 382–388.

DuBois, D. L., & Silverthorn, N. (2005). Natural mentoring relationships and adolescent health: Evidence from a national study. *American Journal of Public Health, 95*(3), 518–524.

Duckworth, A. L., & Seligman, M. P. (2005). Self-discipline outdoes IQ in predicting academic performance of adolescents. *Psychological Science, 16*(12), 939–944.

Duckworth, A. L., & Seligman, M. E. P. (2006). Self-discipline gives girls the edge: Gender in self-discipline, grades, and achievement test scores. *Journal of Educational Psychology, 98*(1), 198–208.

Duyme, M., Dumaret, A.-C., & Tomkiewicz, S. (1999, July 20). How can we boost IQs of "dull children"? A late adoption study. *Proceedings of the National Academy of Sciences of the United States of America, 96*(15), 8790–8794.

Dye, M. W., Green, C. S., & Bavelier, D. (2009). The development of attention skills in action video game players. *Neuropsychologia, 47*(8–9), 1780–1789.

Dye, M. W., Hauser, P. C., & Bavelier, D. (2008, December). Visual skills and cross-modal plasticity in deaf readers: Possible implications for acquiring meaning from print. *Annals of the New York Academy of Sciences, 1145,* 71–82.

Ekman, P. (2003). *Emotions revealed: Recognizing faces and feelings to improve communication and personal life.* New York: Henry Holt.

Emery, R. E., & Laumann-Billings, L. (1998). An overview of the nature, causes, and consequences of abusive family relationships: Toward differentiating maltreatment and violence. *American Psychologist, 53,* 121–135.

Erickson, K., Drevets, W., & Schulkin, J. (2003). Glucocorticoid regulation of diverse cognitive functions in normal and pathological emotional states. *Neuroscience and Biobehavioral Reviews, 27,* 233–246.

Evans, G. W. (2003). A multimethodological analysis of cumulative risk and allostatic load among rural children. *Developmental Psychology, 39*(5), 924–933.

Evans, G. W. (2004). The environment of childhood poverty. *American Psychologist, 59*(2), 77–92.

Evans, G. W., & English, K. (2002). The environment of poverty: Multiple stressor exposure, psychophysiological stress, and socioemotional adjustment. *Child Development, 73*(4), 1238–1248.

Evans, G. W., Gonnella, C., Marcynyszyn, L. A., Gentile, L., & Salpekar, N. (2005). The role of chaos in poverty and children's socioemotional adjustment. *Psychological Science, 16*(7), 560–565.

Evans, G. W., & Kantrowitz, E. (2002, May). Socioeconomic status and health: The potential role of environmental risk exposure. *Annual Review of Public Health, 23,* 303–331.

Evans, G. W., Kim, P., Ting, A. H., Tesher, H. B., & Shannis, D. (2007). Cumulative risk, maternal responsiveness, and allostatic load among young adolescents. *Developmental Psychology, 43*(2), 341–351.

Evans, G. W., Wells, N. M., & Moch, A. (2003). Housing and mental health: A review of the evidence and a methodological and conceptual critique. *Journal of Social Issues, 59*(3), 475–500.

Fabel, K., Fabel, K., Tam, B., Kaufer, D., Baiker, A., Simmons, N., et al. (2003). VEGF is necessary for exercise-induced adult hippocampal neurogenesis. *European Journal of Neuroscience, 18*(10), 2803–2812.

Farah, M. J., Shera, D. M., Savage, J. H., Betancourt, L., Giannetta, J. M., Brodsky, N. L., et al. (2006). Childhood poverty: Specific associations with neurocognitive development. *Brain Research, 1110*(1), 166–174.

Farkas, G. (1998). Reading one-to-one: An intensive program serving a great many students while still achieving large effects. In J. Crane (Ed.), *Social programs that work* (pp. 75–109). New York: Russell Sage Foundation Press.

Farkas, G., & Durham, R. (2007). The role of tutoring in standards-based reform. In A. Gamoran (Ed.), *Standards-based reform and the poverty gap: Lessons for "No Child Left Behind"* (pp. 201–228). Washington, DC: Brookings Institution Press.

Feldman, R., & Eidelman, A. I. (2009). Biological and environmental initial conditions shape the trajectories of cognitive and social-emotional development across the first years of life. *Developmental Science, 12*(1), 194–200.

Felitti, V. J., Anda, R. F., Nordenberg, D., Williamson, D. F., Spitz, A. M., Edwards, V., et al. (1998). Relationship of childhood abuse and household dysfunction to many of the leading causes of death in adults: The Adverse Childhood Experiences (ACE) Study. *American Journal of Preventive Medicine, 14*(4), 245–258.

Felner, R., Jackson, A., Kasak, D., Mulhall, P., Brand, S., & Flowers, N. (1997). The impact of school reform for the middle years: Longitudinal study of a network engaged in Turning Points–based comprehensive school transformation. *Phi Delta Kappan, 78*(7), 528–550.

Ferguson, D. L., & Meyer, G. (2001). *Benito Martinez Elementary, El Paso, TX. Schools on the move: Stories of urban schools engaged in inclusive journeys of change.* Newton, MA: National Institute for Urban School Improvement, Education Development Center Inc.

Finn, J. D., & Achilles, C. M. (1999). Tennessee's class size study: Findings, implications, misconceptions. *Educational Evaluation and Policy Analysis, 21*(2), 97–109.

Fishbein, D. H., Herman-Stahl, M., Eldreth, D., Paschall, M. J., Hyde, C., Hubal, R., et al. (2006). Mediators of the stress-substance-use relationship in urban male adolescents. *Prevention Science, 7*(2), 113–126.

Flynn, J. R. (1984). The mean IQ of Americans: Massive gains 1932 to 1978. *Psychological Bulletin, 95,* 29–51.

Ford, S., Farah, M. S., Shera, D. M., & Hurt, H. (2007). Neurocognitive correlates of problem behavior in environmentally at-risk adolescents. *Journal of Developmental and Behavioral Pediatrics, 28*(5), 376–385.

Freiberg, H. (1993). A school that fosters resilience in inner-city youth. *The Journal of Negro Education, 62*(3), 364.

Gaab, N., Gabrieli, J. D., Deutsch, G. K., Tallal, P., & Temple E. (2007). Neural correlates of rapid auditory processing are disrupted in children with developmental dyslexia and ameliorated with training: An fMRI study. *Neurological Neuroscience, 25*(3–4), 295–310.

Gamoran, A. (Ed.). (2007). *Standards-based reform and the poverty gap: Lessons for "No Child Left Behind."* Washington, DC: Brookings Institution Press.

Gardini, S., Cornoldi, C., De Beni, R., & Venneri, A. (2008, November 6). Cognitive and neuronal processes involved in sequential generation of general and specific mental images. *Psychological Research,* 645–655.

Gazzaniga, M. (Organizer), & Asbury, C., & Rich, B. (Eds.). (2008). *Learning, arts, and the brain: The Dana Consortium report on arts and cognition.* New York & Washington, DC: Dana Press.

Geronimus, A. T., Hicken, M., Keene, D., & Bound, J. (2006). Weathering and age patterns of allostatic load scores among blacks and whites in the United States. *American Journal of Public Health, 96,* 826–833.

Gershoff, E. T. (2002). Corporal punishment by parents and associated child behaviors and experiences: A meta-analytic and theoretical review. *Psychological Bulletin, 128*(4), 539–579.

Giangreco, M. F., Cloninger, C. J., & Iverson, V. S. (1998). *Choosing outcomes and accommodations for children (COACH): A guide to educational planning for students with disabilities* (2nd ed.). Baltimore: Brookes Publishing.

Gobet, F., & Clarkson, G. (2004). Chunks in expert memory: Evidence for the magical number four . . . or is it two? *Memory, 12*(6), 732–747.

Gómez-Pinilla, F., Dao, L., & So, V. (1997). Physical exercise induces FGF-2 and its mRNA in the hippocampus. *Brain Research, 764*(1–2), 1–8.

Gottfredson, L. S. (2004). Intelligence: Is it the epidemiologists' elusive "fundamental cause" of social class inequalities in health? *Journal of Personality and Social Psychology, 86,* 174–199.

Gottfried, A. W., Gottfried, A. E., Bathurst, K., Guerin, D. W., & Parramore, M. M. (2003). Socioeconomic status in children's development and family environment: Infancy through adolescence. In M. H. Bornstein & R. H. Bradley (Eds.), *Socioeconomic status, parenting, and child development* (pp. 260–285). Mahwah, NJ: Lawrence Erlbaum Associates.

Gottlieb, D. J., Beiser, A. S., & O'Connor, G. T. (1995). Poverty, race, and medication use are correlates of asthma hospitalization rates: A small area analysis in Boston. *Chest, 108*(1), 28–35.

Graber, J. A., & Brooks-Gunn, J. (1995). Models of development: Understanding risk in adolescence. *Suicide and Life-Threatening Behavior, 25,* 18–25.

Grassi-Oliveira, R., Ashy, M., & Stein, L. M. (2008). Psychobiology of childhood maltreatment: Effects of allostatic load? *Revista Brasileira de Psiquiatria, 30*(1), 60–68.

Green, R. E., Melo, B., Christensen, B., Ngo, L., & Skene, C. (2006). Evidence of transient enhancement to cognitive functioning in healthy young adults through environmental enrichment: Implications for rehabilitation after brain injury. *Brain and Cognition, 60*(2), 201–203.

Guilarte, T. R., Toscano, C. D., McGlothan, J. L., & Weaver, S. A. (2003). Environmental enrichment reverses cognitive and molecular deficits induced by developmental lead exposure. *Annals of Neurology, 53*(1), 50–56.

Gunnar, M. R., Frenn, K., Wewerka, S. S., & Van Ryzin, M. J. (2009). Moderate versus severe early life stress: Associations with stress reactivity and regulation in 10–12-year-old children. *Psychoneuroendocrinology, 34*(1), 62–75.

Hammack, P. L., Robinson, W. L., Crawford, I., & Li, S. T. (2004). Poverty and depressed mood among urban African-American adolescents: A family stress perspective. *Journal of Child and Family Studies, 13*(3), 309–323.

Hampton, F., Mumford, D., & Bond, L. (1997, March). *Enhancing urban student achievement through family oriented school practices.* Paper presented at the annual meeting of the American Educational Research Association, Chicago, IL.

Harada, C., Harada, T., Mitamura, Y., Quah, H. M., Ohtsuka, K., Kotake, S., et al. (2004, January 15). Diverse NF-kappaB expression in epiretinal membranes after human diabetic retinopathy and proliferative vitreoretinopathy. *Molecular Vision, 10,* 31–36.

Harris, J. R. (1998). *The nurture assumption.* New York: W. H. Norton.

Harris, J. R. (2006). *No two alike.* New York: W. H. Norton.

Hart, B., & Risley, T. (1995). *Meaningful differences in the everyday experiences of young American children.* Baltimore: Brookes Publishing.

Haskins, R. (1989). Beyond metaphor: The efficacy of early childhood education. *American Psychologist, 44*(2), 274–282.

Hawkins, J. D., Guo, J., Hill, K. G., Battin-Pearson, S., & Abbott, R. D. (2001). Long-term effects of the Seattle Social Development Intervention on school bonding trajectories. *Applied Developmental Science, 5*(4), 225–236.

Hawkins, J. D., Kosterman, R., Catalano, R. F., Hill, K. G., & Abbott, R. D. (2008). Effects of Social Development Intervention in childhood 15 years later. *Archives of Pediatrics and Adolescent Medicine, 162*(12), 1133–1141.

Herman, J., & Gribbons, B. (2001). *Lessons learned in using data to support school inquiry and continuous improvement: Final report to the Stuart Foundation.* Los Angeles: Center for the Study of Evaluation.

Herrera, C., Grossman, J. B., Kauh, T. J., Feldman, A. F., & McMaken, J., with Jucovy, L. Z. (2007, August). *Making a difference in schools: The Big Brothers Big Sisters school-based mentoring impact study.* Philadelphia: Public/Private Ventures.

Hill, N. E., Bromell, L., Tyson, D. F., & Flint, R. (2007). Developmental commentary: Ecological perspectives on parental influences during adolescence. *Journal of Clinical Child and Adolescent Psychology, 36*(3), 367–377.

Hillman, C. H., Castelli, D. M., & Buck, S. M. (2005). Aerobic fitness and neurocognitive function in healthy preadolescent children. *Medicine and Science in Sports and Exercise, 37*(11), 1967–1974.

Hoff, E. (2003). The specificity of environmental influence: Socioeconomic status affects early vocabulary development via maternal speech. *Child Development, 74*(5), 1368–1378.

Hoffman, A. M. (1996). *Schools, violence, and society.* Westport, CT: Praeger Publishers.

Hsuch, J., & Yoshikawa, H. (2007). Working nonstandard schedules and variable shifts in low-income families: Associations with parental psychological well-being, family functioning, and child well-being. *Developmental Psychology, 43*(3), 620–632.

Hussey, J. M., Chang, J. J., & Kotch, J. B. (2006). Child maltreatment in the United States: Prevalence, risk factors, and adolescent health consequences. *Pediatrics, 118*(3), 933–942.

Huttenlocher, J. (1998). Language input and language growth. *Preventive Medicine, 27*(2), 195–199.

Huttenlocher, J., Haight, W., Bryk, A., Seltzer, M., & Lyons, R. (1991). Early vocabulary growth: Relation to language input and gender. *Developmental Psychology, 27*(2), 236–248.

Isaacs, E. B., Gadian, D. G., Sabatini, S., Chong, W. K., Quinn, B. T., Fischl, B. R., et al. (2008). The effect of early human diet on caudate volumes and IQ. *Pediatric Research, 63*(3), 308–314.

Izawa, C. (2000). Total time and efficient time management: In search of optimal learning and retention via study-test-rest presentation programs. *American Journal of Psychology, 113*(2), 221–248.

Jack, G., & Jordan, B. (1999). Social capital and child welfare. *Children and Society, 13,* 242–256.

Jaeggi, S. M., Buschkuehl, M., Jonides, J., & Perrig, W. J. (2008). Improving fluid intelligence with training on working memory. *Proceedings of the National Academy of Sciences of the United States of America, 105*(19), 6829–6833.

Jekielek, S., Moore, K. A., & Hair, E. (2002, February). *Mentoring: A promising strategy for youth development. Child Trends* [research brief]. Available: www.mentoring.ca.gov/pdf/MentoringBrief2002.pdf

Jensen, E. (2003). *Tools for engagement.* Thousand Oaks, CA: Corwin Press.

Jensen, E. (2005). *Teaching with the brain in mind.* Alexandria, VA: ASCD.

Jensen, E., & Nickelsen, L. (2008). *Deeper learning: 7 powerful strategies for in-depth and longer-lasting learning.* Thousand Oaks, CA: Corwin Press.

Jerald, C. D. (2001). *Dispelling the myth revisited: Preliminary findings from a nationwide analysis of "high-flying" schools.* Washington, DC: The Education Trust.

Jiaxu, C., & Weiyi, Y. (2000). Influence of acute and chronic treadmill exercise on rat brain POMC gene expression. *Medicine and Science in Sports and Exercise, 32*(5), 954–957.

Johns, M., Schmader, T., & Martens, A. (2005). Knowing is half the battle: Teaching stereotype threat as a means of improving women's math performance. *Psychological Science, 16,* 175–179.

Johnson, D. S. (1981). Naturally acquired learned helplessness: The relationship of school failure to achievement behavior, attributions, and self-concept. *Journal of Educational Psychology, 73*(2), 174–180.

Johnston-Brooks, C. H., Lewis, M. A., Evans, G. W., & Whalen, C. K. (1998). Chronic stress and illness in children: The role of allostatic load. *Psychosomatic Medicine, 60*(5), 597–603.

Jolliffe, D. (2004, July 20). *Rural poverty at a glance.* Rural Development Research Report Number 100. Washington, DC: Economic Research Service, U.S. Department of Agriculture. Retrieved June 10, 2009, from www.ers.usda.gov/Publications/RDRR100

Jones, B., Valdez, G., Nowakowski, J., & Rasmussen, C. (1994). *Designing learning and technology for educational reform.* Oak Brook, IL: North Central Regional Educational Laboratory.

Jonides, J. (2008). Musical skill and cognition. In M. Gazzaniga (Organizer) & C. Asbury & B. Rich (Eds.), *Learning, arts, and the brain: The Dana Consortium report on arts and cognition* (pp. 11–16). New York & Washington, DC: Dana Press.

Jordan, H., Mendro, R., & Weerasinghe, D. (1997). *Teacher effects on longitudinal student achievement: A report on research in progress.* Paper presented at the annual CREATE meeting, Indianapolis, IN.

Joseph, R. (1999). Environmental influences on neural plasticity, the limbic system, emotional development and attachment: A review. *Child Psychiatry and Human Development, 29*(**3**), 189–208.

Jyoti, D. F., Frongillo, E. A., & Jones, S. J. (2005, December). Food insecurity affects school children's academic performance, weight gain, and social skills. *Journal of Nutrition, 135,* 2831–2839.

Kam, C., Greenberg, M., & Walls, C. (2003). Examining the role of implementation quality in school-based prevention using the PATHS curriculum. *Prevention Science, 4*(1).

Kanaya, T., Scullin, M. H., & Ceci, S. J. (2003). The Flynn effect and U.S. policies: The impact of rising IQ scores on American society via mental retardation diagnoses. *American Psychologist, 58*(10), 778–790.

Kandel, E. (1998, April). A new intellectual framework for psychiatry? *The American Journal of Psychiatry, 155,* 457–469.

Kannapel, P. J., & Clements, S. K., with Taylor, D., & Hibpshman, T. (2005). *Inside the black box of high-performing high-poverty schools.* Lexington, KY: Prichard Committee for Academic Excellence.

Karpicke, J. D., & Roediger, H. L. (2008). The critical importance of retrieval for learning. *Science, 319*(5865), 966–968.

Keegan-Eamon, M., & Zuehl, R. M. (2001). Maternal depression and physical punishment as mediators of the effect of poverty on socioemotional problems of children in single-mother families. *American Journal of Orthopsychiatry, 71*(2), 218–226.

Kearney, J. A. (1997). Emotional development in infancy: Theoretical models and nursing implications. *Journal of Child and Adolescent Psychiatric Nursing, 10*(4), 7–17.

Kerns, K. A., Eso, K., & Thomson, J. (1999). Investigation of a direct intervention for improving attention in young children with ADHD. *Developmental Neuropsychology, 16*(2), 273–295.

King, K., Vidourek, R., Davis, B., & McClellan, W. (2002). Increasing self-esteem and school connectedness through a multidimensional mentoring program. *Journal of School Health, 72*(7), 294–299.

Kirkpatrick, L. A., & Ellis, B. J. (2001). An evolutionary-psychological approach to self-esteem: Multiple domains and multiple functions. In G. J. O. Fletcher & M. S. Clark (Eds.), *Blackwell handbook of social psychology: Interpersonal processes* (pp. 411–436). Malden, MA: Blackwell.

Klebanov, P., & Brooks-Gunn, J. (2006, December). Cumulative, human capital, and psychological risk in the context of early intervention: Links with IQ at ages 3, 5, and 8. *Annals of the New York Academy of Sciences, 1094,* 63–82.

Klingberg, T. (2000). Limitations in information processing in the human brain: Neuroimaging of dual task performance and working memory tasks. *Progress in Brain Research, 126,* 95–102.

Klingberg, T., Fernell, E., Olesen, P. J., Johnson, M., Gustafsson, P., Dahlström, K., et al. (2005). Computerized training of working memory in children with ADHD—A randomized, controlled trial. *Journal of the American Academy of Child and Adolescent Psychiatry, 44*(2), 177–186.

Klopfenstein, K. (2004). Advanced placement: Do minorities have equal opportunity? *Economics of Education Review, 23*(2), 115–131.

Koger, S. M., Schettler, T., & Weiss, B. (2005). Environmental toxicants and developmental disabilities: A challenge for psychologists. *American Psychologist, 60*(3), 243–255.

Kovas, Y., Haworth, C. M., Harlaar, N., Petrill, S. A., Dale, P. S., & Plomin, R. (2007). Overlap and specificity of genetic and environmental influences on mathematics and reading disability in 10-year-old twins. *Journal of Child Psychology and Psychiatry, 48*(9), 914–922.

Kretovics, J., Farber, K. S., & Armaline, W. D. (2004). It ain't brain surgery: Reconstructing schools to improve the education of children placed at risk. *Educational Horizons, 82*(3), 213–225.

Kumanyika, S., & Grier, S. (2006). Targeting interventions for ethnic minority and low-income populations. *Future Child, 16*(1), 187–207.

Lachat, M., & Smith, S. (2005). Practices that support data use in urban high schools. *Journal of Education for Students Placed at Risk (JESPAR), 10*(3), 333–349.

Lave, J. (1988). *Cognition in practice.* New York: Cambridge University Press.

Lee, V., & Burkam, D. (2003). Dropping out of high school: The role of school organization and structure. *American Educational Research Journal, 40*(2), 353–393.

Lengler, R., & Eppler, M. (2007). *Towards a periodic table of visualization methods for management.* IASTED proceedings of the Conference on Graphics and Visualization in Engineering (GVE 2007), Clearwater, FL.

Leroux, C., & Grossman, R. (1999, October 21). Arts in the schools paint masterpiece: Higher scores. *Chicago Tribune,* p. A-1.

Levenson, C. W., & Rich, N. J. (2007). Eat less, live longer? New insights into the role of caloric restriction in the brain. *Nutrition Reviews, 65*(9), 412–415.

Lewis, A. (1993, June). The payoff from a quality preschool. *Phi Delta Kappan, 74,* 746–749.

Liaw, F. R., & Brooks-Gunn, J. (1994). Cumulative familial risks and low-birthweight children's cognitive and behavioral development. *Journal of Clinical Child Psychology, 23*(4), 360–372.

Lichter, D. T. (1997, August). Poverty and inequality among children. *Annual Review of Sociology, 23,* 121–145.

Lippman, L., Burns, S., & McArthur, E. (1996). *Urban schools: The challenge of location and poverty*. Washington, DC: U.S. Department of Education, Office of Educational Research and Improvement.

Love, J. M., et al. (2005). The effectiveness of Early Head Start for 3-year-old children and their parents: Lessons for policy and programs. *Developmental Psychology, 41*(6), 885–901.

Love, J. M., Kisker, E. E., Ross, C. M., Schochet, P. Z., Brooks-Gunn, J., Paulsell, D., et al. (2002). *Making a difference in the lives of infants and toddlers and their families: The impacts of Early Head Start. Volume I: Final technical report*. Princeton, NJ: Mathematica Policy Research Inc.

Lucey, P. (2007). Social determinates of health. *Nursing Economics, 25*(2), 103–109.

Lupien, S. J., King, S., Meaney, M. J., & McEwen, B. S. (2001). Can poverty get under your skin? Basal cortisol levels and cognitive function in children from low and high socioeconomic status. *Developmental Psychopathology, 13*(3), 653–676.

Maguire, E. A., Spiers, H. J., Good, C. D., Hartley, T., Frackowiak, R. S., & Burgess, N. (2003). Navigation expertise and the human hippocampus: A structural brain imaging analysis. *Hippocampus, 13*(2), 250–259.

Margulies, S. (1991). *The effect of chess on reading scores: District Nine Chess Program second year report*. New York: The American Chess Foundation. Available: www.geocities.com/chess_camp/margulies.pdf

Marzano, R. J. (2004). *Building background knowledge for academic achievement: Research on What Works in School*. Alexandria, VA: ASCD.

Marzano, R. J. (2007). *The art and science of teaching*. Alexandria, VA: ASCD.

Marzano, R. J., Pickering, D. J., & Pollock, J. E. (2001). *Classroom instruction that works*. Alexandria, VA: ASCD.

Maslow, A. H. (1943). A theory of human motivation. *Psychological Review, 50,* 370–396.

Matte, T. D., & Jacobs, D. E. (2000). Housing and health—Current issues and implications for research and programs. *Journal of Urban Health, 77*(1), 7–25.

May, A. (2008). Chronic pain may change the structure of the brain. *Pain, 137,* 7–15.

McCauley, D. S. (2007). *The impact of advanced placement and dual enrollment programs on college graduation*. Research report. San Marcos, TX: Texas State University–San Marcos. Retrieved June 30, 2008, from http://ecommons.txstate.edu/arp/206

McCoy, M. B., Frick, P. J., Loney, B. R., & Ellis, M. L. (1999). The potential mediating role of parenting practices in the development of conduct problems in a clinic-referred sample. *Journal of Child and Family Studies, 8*(4), 477–494.

McLoyd, V. C. (1998). Socioeconomic disadvantage and child development. *American Psychologist, 53*(2), 185–204.

Mehan, H., Villanueva, I., Hubbard, L., & Lintz, A. (1996). *Constructing school success: The consequences of untracking low-achieving students*. Cambridge, UK: Cambridge University Press.

Mehrabian, A. (2002). Beyond IQ: Broad-based measurement of individual success potential or "emotional intelligence." *Genetic, Social, & General Psychology Monographs, 126*(2), 133–239.

Meinzer, M., Elbert, T., Wienbruch, C., Djundja, D., Barthel, G., & Rockstroh, B. (2004, August). Intensive language training enhances brain plasticity in chronic aphasia. *BMC Biology, 2,* 20.

Menyuk, P. (1980). Effect of persistent otitis media on language development. *Annals of Otology, Rhinology, and Laryngology Supplement, 89*(3), 257–263.

Mid-continent Research for Education and Learning (McREL). (2005). Schools that "beat the odds." *McREL Insights.* Aurora, CO: Author. Retrieved June 28, 2008, from www.mcrel.org/PDF/SchoolImprovementReform/5051IR_Beat_the_odds.pdf

Mikulincer, M., & Shaver, R. (2001, July). Attachment theory and intergroup bias: Evidence that priming the secure base schema attenuates negative reactions to out-groups. *Journal of Personality and Social Psychology, 81,* 97–115.

Miller, A. L., Seifer, R., Stroud, L., Sheinkopf, S. J., & Dickstein, S. (2006, December). Biobehavioral indices of emotion regulation relate to school attitudes, motivation, and behavior problems in a low-income preschool sample. *Annals of the New York Academy of Sciences, 1094,* 325–329.

Miller, L. B., & Bizzell, R. P. (1984). Long-term effects of four preschool programs: Ninth- and tenth-grade results. *Child Development, 55*(4), 1570–1587.

Milne, A., & Plourde, L. A. (2006). Factors of a low-SES household: What aids academic achievement? *Journal of Instructional Psychology, 33*(3), 183–193.

Morrison-Gutman, L., & McLoyd, V. (2000). Parents' management of their children's education within the home, at school, and in the community: An examination of African-American families living in poverty. *The Urban Review, 32*(1), 1–24.

Moses, M., Johnson, E. S., Anger, W. K., Burse, V. W., Horstman, S. W., Jackson, R. J., et al. (1993). Environmental equity and pesticide exposure. *Toxicology and Industrial Health, 9*(5), 913–959.

Mouton, S. G., & Hawkins, J. (1996). School attachment perspectives of low-attached high school students. *Educational Psychology, 16*(3), 297–304.

Murray, A. (1997). Young people without an upper secondary education in Sweden: Their home background, school and labour market experiences. *Scandinavian Journal of Educational Research, 41*(2), 93–125.

National Commission on Teaching and America's Future (NCTAF). (2004). 2004 Summit on High Quality Teacher Preparation. Available: www.nctaf.org/resources/events/2004_summit-1

National Education Association (NEA). (2003, Spring). *Using data about classroom practice and student work to improve professional development for educators.* Washington, DC: The NEA Foundation for the Improvement of Education. Available: www.neafoundation.org/downloads/NEA-Using_Date_Classroom_Practice.pdf

Newcomer, J. W., Selke, G., Melson, A. K., Hershey, T., Craft, S., Richards, K., et al. (1999). Decreased memory performance in healthy humans induced by stress-level cortisol treatment. *Archives of General Psychiatry, 56*(6), 527–533.

Newman, T. (2005, Spring). Coaches' roles in the academic success of male student athletes. *The Sport Journal,* 8.

Nithianantharajah, J., & Hannan, A. J. (2006). Enriched environments, experience-dependent plasticity and disorders of the nervous system. *Nature Reviews Neuroscience, 7*(9), 697–709.

Noble, K. G., McCandliss, B. D., & Farah, M. J. (2007). Socioeconomic gradients predict individual differences in neurocognitive abilities. *Developmental Science, 10*(4), 464–480.

Noble, K. G., Norman, M. F., & Farah, M. J. (2005, January). Neurocognitive correlates of socioeconomic status in kindergarten children. *Developmental Science, 8*(1), 74–87.

Noble, K. G., Wolmetz, M. E., Ochs, L. G., Farah, M. J., & McCandliss, B. D. (2006, November). Brain-behavior relationships in reading acquisition are modulated by socioeconomic factors. *Developmental Science, 9*(6), 642–654.

Nye, B., Konstantopoulos, S., & Hedges, L. V. (2004). How large are teacher effects? *Educational Evaluation and Policy Analysis, 26*(3), 237–257.

Oden, S., Schweinhart, L., & Weikart, D. (2000). *Into adulthood: A study of the effects of Head Start*. Ypsilanti, MI: High/Scope Press.

Palmer, L. L., Giese, L., & DeBoer, B. (2008). *Early literacy champions in North Carolina: Accelerated learning documentation for K–3 SMART (Stimulating Maturity through Accelerated Readiness Training)*. Minneapolis, MN: Minnesota Learning Resource Center.

Parrett, W. H. (2005). Against all odds: Reversing low achievement of one school's Native American students. *School Administrator, 62*(1), 26.

Pascual-Leone, A., Amedi, A., Fregni, F., & Merabet, L. B. (2005). The plastic human brain cortex. *Annual Review of Neuroscience, 28,* 377–401.

Paulussen-Hoogeboom, M. C., Stams, G. J., Hermanns, J. M. A., & Peetsma, T. T. D. (2007). Child negative emotionality and parenting from infancy to preschool: A meta-analytic review. *Journal of Youth and Adolescence, 37*(7), 875–887.

Peden, A. R., Rayens, M. K., Hall, L. A., & Grant, E. (2005). Testing an intervention to reduce negative thinking, depressive symptoms, and chronic stressors in low-income single mothers. *Journal of Nursing Scholarship, 37*(3), 268–274.

Pellegrini, A. D., & Bohn, C. M. (2005). The role of recess in children's cognitive performance and school adjustment. *Educational Researcher, 34*(1), 13–19.

Pereira, A. C., Huddleston, D. E., Brickman, A. M., Sosunov, A. A., Hen, R., McKhann, G. M., et al. (2007). An *in vivo* correlate of exercise-induced neurogenesis in the adult dentate gyrus. *Proceedings of the National Academy of Sciences of the United States of America, 104*(13), 5638–5643.

Peterson, C., Maier, S. F., & Seligman, M. E. P. (1995). *Learned helplessness: A theory for the age of personal control*. New York: Oxford University Press.

Pianta, R. C., Belsky, J., Houts, R., & Morrison, F. (2007). Teaching: Opportunities to learn in America's elementary classrooms. *Science, 315*(5820), 1795–1796.

Pianta, R. C., & Stuhlman, M. (2004). Teacher-child relationships and children's success in the first years of school. *School Psychology Review, 33*(3), 444–458.

Plomin, R., & Kovas, Y. (2005). Generalist genes and learning disabilities. *Psychological Bulletin, 131*(4), 592–617.

Popham, W. J. (2004). A game without winners. *Educational Leadership, 62*(3), 46–50.

Popham, W. J. (2008). *Transformative assessment*. Alexandria, VA: ASCD.

Poplin, M., & Soto-Hinman, I. (2006). Taking off ideological blinders: Lessons from the start of a study on effective teachers in high-poverty schools. *The Journal of Education, 186*(3), 41–44.

Posner, M. I. (2008). Measuring alertness. *Annals of the New York Academy of Sciences, 1129,* 193–199.

Posner, M., Rothbart, M. K., Sheese, B. E., & Kieras, J. (2008). How arts training influences cognition. In M. Gazzaniga (Organizer) & C. Asbury & B. Rich (Eds.), *Learning, arts, and the brain: The Dana Consortium report on arts and cognition* (pp. 1–10). New York & Washington, DC: Dana Press.

Pratt, P., Tallis, F., & Eysenck, M. (1997). Information-processing, storage characteristics and worry. *Behavior Research & Therapy, 35*(11), 1015–1023.

Ramey, C. T., & Campbell, F. A. (1991). Poverty, early childhood education, and academic competence: The Abecedarian experiment. In A. C. Huston (Ed.), *Children in poverty:*

Child development and public policy (pp. 190–221). Cambridge, UK: Cambridge University Press.

Ramey, C., & Ramey, S. (1998). Prevention of intellectual disabilities: Early interventions to improve cognitive development. *Preventive Medicine, 27*, 224–232.

Ramey, C. T., & Ramey, S. L. (2006). Early learning and school readiness: Can early intervention make a difference? In N. F. Watt, C. C. Ayoub, R. H. Bradley, J. E. Puma, & W. A. Lebeouf (Eds.), *The crisis in youth mental health: Critical issues and effective programs, vol. 4: Early intervention programs and policies* (pp. 291–317). Westport, CT: Praeger Press.

Ratey, J., & Hagerman, E. (2008). *Spark: The revolutionary new science of exercise and the brain.* Boston: Little, Brown & Company.

Rector, R. E. (2005). *Importing poverty: Immigration and poverty in the United States: A book of charts (Special Report #9).* Washington, DC: The Heritage Foundation.

Reeve, J. (2006). Extrinsic rewards and inner motivation. In C. Evertson, C. M. Weinstein, & C. S. Weinstein (Eds.), *Handbook of classroom management: Research, practice and contemporary issues* (pp. 645–664). Mahwah, NJ: Lawrence Erlbaum Associates.

Reeves, D. B. (2003). *High performance in high poverty schools: 90/90/90 and beyond.* Denver, CO: Center for Performance Assessment.

Rogers, D. E., & Ginzberg, E. (1993). *Medical care and the health of the poor.* Boulder, CO: Westview Press.

Rosenthal, R., & Jacobson, L. (1992). *Pygmalion in the classroom: Teacher expectation and pupils' intellectual development* (Expanded ed.). New York: Irvington.

Rushton, J. P. (2000). Flynn effects not genetic and unrelated to race differences. *American Psychologist, 55*(5), 542–543.

Rutter, M., Moffitt, T. E., & Caspi, A. (2006). Gene-environment interplay and psychopathology: Multiple varieties but real effects. *Journal of Child Psychology and Psychiatry, 47*(3–4), 226–261.

Sallis, J., McKenzie, T., Kolody, B., Lewis, M., Marshall, S., & Rosengard, P. (1999). Effects of health-related physical education on academic achievement: Project SPARK. *Research Quarterly for Exercise and Sport, 70*(2), 127–134.

Sameroff, A. (1998). Environmental risk factors in infancy. *Pediatrics, 102*(5), 1287–1292.

Sampson, R. J., Raudenbush, S. W., & Earls, F. (1997, August 15). Neighborhoods and violent crime: A multilevel study of collective efficacy. *Science, 277*, 918–924.

Sanborn, K. J., Truscott, S. D., Phelps, L., & McDougal, J. L. (2003). Does the Flynn effect differ by IQ level in samples of students classified as learning disabled? *Journal of Psychoeducational Assessment, 21*(2), 145–159.

Sanders, W. L., & Rivers, J. C. (1996). *Cumulative and residual effects of teachers on future student academic achievement.* Knoxville, TN: University of Tennessee Value-Added Research and Assessment Center.

Sapolsky, R. (2005). Sick of poverty. *Scientific American, 293*(6), 92–99.

Sargent, D., Brown, M. J., Freeman, J. L., Bailey, A., Goodman, D., & Freeman, D. H., Jr. (1995). Childhood lead poisoning in Massachusetts communities: Its association with sociodemographic and housing characteristics. *American Journal of Public Health, 85*(4), 528–534.

Saudino, K. J. (2005). Behavioral genetics and child temperament. *Journal of Developmental and Behavioral Pediatrics, 26*(3), 214–223.

Schafft, K. A. (2006). Poverty, residential mobility, and student transiency within a rural New York school district. *Rural Sociology, 71*(2), 212–231.

Schinke, S. P., Cole, K. C., & Poulin, S. R. (2000). Enhancing the educational achievement of at-risk youth. *Prevention Science, 1*(1), 51–60.

Schmoker, M. (2001). *The results fieldbook: Practical strategies from dramatically improved schools.* Alexandria, VA: ASCD.

Schmoker, M. (2002). Up and away. *Journal of Staff Development, 23*(2), 10–13.

Schwartz, D., & Gorman, A. H. (2003). Community violence exposure and children's academic functioning. *Journal of Educational Psychology, 95*(1), 163–173.

Schwartz, J. (1994). Low-level lead exposure and children's IQ: A meta-analysis and search for a threshold. *Environmental Research, 65*(1), 42–55.

Schweinhart, L. J., Barnes, H. V., & Weikart, D. P. (1993). *Significant benefits: The High/Scope Perry Preschool Study through age 27.* (Monographs of the High/Scope Educational Research Foundation). Ypsilanti, MI: High/Scope Press.

Segawa, M. (2008). Development of intellect, emotion, and intentions, and their neuronal systems. *Brain and Nerve, 60*(9), 1009–1016.

Seligman, M. E., & Csikszentmihalyi, M. (2000). Positive psychology: An introduction. *American Psychologist, 55*(1), 5–14.

Shaywitz, S. E., Shaywitz, B. A., Pugh, K. R., Fulbright, R. K., Constable, R. T., Mencl, W. E., et al. (1998). Functional disruption in the organization of the brain for reading in dyslexia. *Proceedings of the National Academy of Sciences of the United States of America, 95*(5), 2636–2641.

Sibley, B. A., & Etnier, J. L. (2003). The relationship between physical activity and cognition in children: A meta-analysis. *Pediatric Exercise Science, 15,* 243–256.

Simoes, E. A. (2003). Environmental and demographic risk factors for respiratory syncytial virus lower respiratory tract disease. *Journal of Pediatrics, 143,* S118–S126.

Sinclair, J. J., Pettit, G. S., Harrist, A. W., Dodge, K. A., & Bates, J. E. (1994). Encounters with aggressive peers in early childhood: Frequency, age differences and correlates of risk for behavior problems. *International Journal of Behavioral Development, 17,* 675–696.

Skeels, H. M. (1966). Adult status of children with contrasting early life experiences: A follow-up study. *Monographs of the Society for Research in Child Development, 31*(3), 1–65.

Slack, K. S., Holl, J. L., McDaniel, M., Yoo, J., & Bolger, K. (2004). Understanding the risks of child neglect: An exploration of poverty and parenting characteristics. *Child Maltreatment, 9*(4), 395–408.

Slater, P. (2003, January 28). *State schools chief O'Connell announces California kids' 2002 physical fitness results.* California Department of Education. Retrieved July 8, 2007, from www.cde.ca.gov/nr/ne/yr03/yr03rel07.asp

Slavin, R. E., & Calderon, M. (2001). *Effective programs for Latino students.* Mahwah, NJ: Lawrence Erlbaum Associates.

Smith, J. R., Brooks-Gunn, J., & Klebanov, P. K. (1997). Consequences of living in poverty for young children's cognitive and verbal ability and early school achievement. In G. Duncan & J. Brooks-Gunn (Eds.), *Consequences of growing up poor* (pp. 132–189). New York: Russell Sage Foundation.

Sowell, E. R., Peterson, B. S., Thompson, P. M., Welcome, S. E., Henkenius, A. L., & Toga, A. W. (2003). Mapping cortical change across the human life span. *Nature Neuroscience, 6*(3), 309–315.

Spelke, E. (2008). Effects of music instruction on developing cognitive systems at the foundations of mathematics and science. In M. Gazzaniga (Organizer) & C. Asbury & B. Rich

(Eds.), *Learning, arts, and the brain: The Dana Consortium report on arts and cognition* (pp. 17–50). New York & Washington, DC: Dana Press.

Sroufe, A. L. (2005). Attachment and development: A prospective, longitudinal study from birth to adulthood. *Attachment and Human Development, 7*(4), 349–367.

Stewart, L. (2008). Do musicians have different brains? *Clinical Medicine, 8*(3), 304–308.

Stipek, D. J. (2001). *Pathways to constructive lives: The importance of early school success.* Washington, DC: American Psychological Association.

Strong, R., Silver, H., & Perini, M. (2001). *Teaching what matters most: Standards and strategies for raising student achievement.* Alexandria, VA: ASCD.

Sutoo, D., & Akiyama, K. (2003). The significance of increase in striatal D(2) receptors in epileptic EL mice. *Brain Research, 980*(1), 24–30.

Szanton, S. L., Gill, J. M., & Allen, J. K. (2005). Allostatic load: A mechanism of socioeconomic health disparities? *Biological Research for Nursing, 7*(1), 7–15.

Szewczyk-Sokolowski, M., Bost, K. K., & Wainwright, A. B. (2005, August). Attachment, temperament, and preschool children's peer acceptance. *Social Development, 14,* 379–397.

Temple, E., Deutsch, G. K., Poldrack, R. A., Miller, S. L., Tallal, P., Merzenich, M. M., et al. (2003). Neural deficits in children with dyslexia ameliorated by behavioral remediation: Evidence from functional MRI. *Proceedings of the National Academy of Sciences of the United States of America, 100*(5), 2860–2865.

Teutsch, S., Herken, W., Bingel, U., Schoell, E., & May, A. (2008). Changes in brain gray matter due to repetitive painful stimulation. *Neuroimage, 42*(2), 845–849.

Tiberius, R., & Tipping, J. (1990). *Twelve principles of effective teaching and learning for which there is substantial empirical support.* Toronto, Canada: University of Toronto.

Todd, J. J., & Marois, R. (2004). Capacity limit of visual short-term memory in human posterior parietal cortex. *Nature, 428*(6984), 751–754.

Tong, S., Baghurst, P., Vimpani, G., & McMichael, A. (2007). Socioeconomic position, maternal IQ, home environment, and cognitive development. *Journal of Pediatrics, 151*(3), 284–288.

Tremblay, R. E., Vitaro, F., & Brendgen, M. (2000). Influence of deviant friends on delinquency: Searching for moderator variables. *Journal of Abnormal Child Psychology, 28,* 313–325.

Turkheimer, E., Haley, A., Waldron, M., D'Onofrio, B., & Gottesman, I. I. (2003, November). Socioeconomic status modifies heritability of IQ in young children. *Psychological Science, 14*(6), 623–628.

U.S. Census Bureau. (2000). *National household education survey.* Washington, DC: National Center for Education Statistics.

U.S. Census Bureau. (2006, August 29). Income climbs, poverty stabilizes, uninsured rate increases. Retrieved June 10, 2009, from www.census.gov/Press-Release/www/releases/archives/income_wealth/007419.html

U.S. Department of Education. (2006). Learning from nine high poverty, high achieving Blue Ribbon schools. Retrieved May 21, 2009, from www.ed.gov/programs/nclbbrs/2006/profiles

U.S. Department of Health and Human Services. (2000). *Trends in the well-being of America's children and youth.* Washington, DC: Author.

U.S. News & World Report. (2008, December 4). Best high schools: Gold medal list. Retrieved May 21, 2009, from www.usnews.com/articles/education/high-schools/2008/12/04/best-high-schools-gold-medal-list.html van Ijzendoorn, M. H., Vereijken, C. M. J. L., Bakermans-Kranenburg, M. J., & Riksen-Walraven, M. J. (2004). Assessing attachment security with the attachment q sort: Meta-analytic evidence for the validity of the observer AQS. *Child Development, 75*(4), 1188–1213.

van Praag, H., Kempermann, G., & Gage, F. H. (1999). Running increases cell proliferation and neurogenesis in the adult mouse dentate gyrus. *Nature Neuroscience, 2*(3), 266–270.

Viadero, D. (2002, June 5). Study finds social barriers to advanced classes. *Education Week*, p. 5.

Viadero, D. (2008, February 13). Exercise seen as priming pump for students' academic strides: Case grows stronger for physical activity's link to improved brain function. *Education Week*, pp. 1, 3.

Vythilingam, M., Heim, C., Newport, J., Miller, A. H., Anderson, E., Bronen, R., et al. (2002). Childhood trauma associated with smaller hippocampal volume in women with major depression. *American Journal of Psychiatry, 159*(12), 2072–2080.

Wadsworth, M. E., Raviv, T., Compas, B. E., & Connor-Smith, J. K. (2005). Parent and adolescent responses to poverty-related stress: Tests of mediated and moderated coping models. *Journal of Child and Family Studies, 14*(2), 283–298.

Wagner, M. (1997). *The effects of isotonic resistance exercise on aggression variable in adult male inmates in the Texas Department of Criminal Justice.* Doctoral dissertation, Texas A & M University, College Station.

Wahlsten, D. (1997). The malleability of intelligence is not constrained by heritability. In B. Devlin, S. E. Feinberg, D. P. Resnick, & K. Roeder (Eds.), *Intelligence, genes, and success: Scientists respond to* The Bell Curve (pp. 71–87). New York: Springer.

Wandell, B., Dougherty, R., Ben-Shachar, M., & Deutsch, G. (2008). Training in the arts, reading, and brain imaging. In M. Gazzaniga (Organizer) & C. Asbury & B. Rich (Eds.), *Learning, arts, and the brain: The Dana Consortium report on arts and cognition* (pp. 51–60). New York & Washington, DC: Dana Press.

Wang, Y., & Zhang, Q. (2006). Are American children and adolescents of low socioeconomic status at increased risk of obesity? Changes in the association between overweight and family income between 1971 and 2002. *American Journal of Clinical Nutrition, 84*, 707–716.

Weaver, I. C., Cervoni, N., Champagne, F. A., D'Alessio, A. C., Sharma, S., Seckl, J. R., et al. (2004). Epigenetic programming by maternal behavior. *Nature Neuroscience, 7*(8), 847–854.

Weikart, D. P. (1998). Changing early childhood development through educational intervention. *Preventive Medicine, 27*(2), 233–237.

Weizman, Z. O., & Snow, C. E. (2001). Lexical input as related to children's vocabulary acquisition: Effects of sophisticated exposure and support for meaning. *Developmental Psychology, 37*(2), 265–279.

Welsh, P. (2006, September 19). Students aren't interchangeable. *USA Today*, p. 9.

Westerberg, H., & Klingberg, T. (2007). Changes in cortical activity after training of working memory—A single-subject analysis. *Physiology & Behavior, 92*(1–2), 186–192.

Whitener, L. A., Gibbs, R., & Kusmin, L. (2003, June). Rural welfare reform: Lessons learned. *Amber Waves.* Washington, DC: Economic Research Service, U.S. Department of Agriculture. Retrieved May 21, 2009, from www.ers.usda.gov/AmberWaves/June03/Features/RuralWelfareReforme.htm

Wiggins, G., & McTighe, J. (2005). *Understanding by design.* Alexandria, VA: ASCD.

Williams, T., et al. (2005, October). *Similar students, different results: Why do some schools do better? A large-scale survey of California elementary schools serving low-income students.* Mountain View, CA: EdSource.

Williams, W. M., Blythe, T., White, N., Li, J., Gardner, H., & Sternberg, R. J. (2002). Applying psychological theories to educational practice. *Psychological Science, 6,* 623–628.

Winship, C., & Korenman, S. (1997). Does staying in school make you smarter? The effect of education on IQ in *The Bell Curve.* In B. Devlin, S. E. Feinberg, D. P. Resnick, & K. Roeder (Eds.), *Intelligence, genes, and success: Scientists respond to* The Bell Curve (pp. 215–234). New York: Springer.

Wommack, J. C., & Delville, Y. (2004). Behavioral and neuroendocrine adaptations to repeated stress during puberty in male golden hamsters. *Journal of Neuroendocrinology, 16*(9), 767–775.

Wood, C. (2002). Changing the pace of school: Slowing down the day to improve the quality of learning. *Phi Delta Kappan, 83*(7), 545–550.

Wright, A. J., Nichols, T. R., Graber, J. A., Brooks-Gunn, J., & Botvin, G. J. (2004). It's not what you say, it's how many different ways you can say it: Links between divergent peer resistance skills and delinquency a year later. *Journal of Adolescent Health, 35*(5), 380–391.

Yang, Y., Cao, J., Xiong, W., Zhang, J., Zhou, Q., Wei, H., et al. (2003). Both stress experience and age determine the impairment or enhancement effect of stress on spatial memory retrieval. *Journal of Endocrinology, 178*(1), 45–54.

Yazzie-Mintz, E. (2007). *Voices of students on engagement: A report on the 2006 High School Survey of Student Engagement.* Bloomington, IN: Center for Evaluation and Education Policy, Indiana University.

Zhang, S. Y., & Carrasquillo, A. (1995). Chinese parents' influence on academic performance. *New York State Association for Bilingual Education Journal, 10,* 46–53.

Zohar, A., Degani, A., & Vaaknin, E. (2001). Teachers' beliefs about low-achieving students and higher order thinking. *Teaching and Teacher Education, 17*(4), 469–485.

Zuena, A. R., Mairesse, J., Casolini, P., Cinque, C., Alemà, G. S., Morley-Fletcher, S., et al. (2008). Prenatal restraint stress generates two distinct behavioral and neurochemical profiles in male and female rats. *PLoS ONE, 3*(5), e2170.

Index

note: page numbers followed by f refer to figures.

About the Author

Eric Jensen is a former teacher with a real love of learning. He has taught at all levels, from elementary school through university, and he is currently completing his Ph.D. in human development. In 1981, Jensen cofounded the United States' first and largest brain-compatible learning program, now with more than 50,000 graduates. He has since written *Teaching with the Brain in Mind, Brain-Based Learning, Enriching the Brain,* and 25 other books on learning and the brain. A leader in the brain-based movement, he has made more than 65 visits to neuroscience labs and interacts with dozens of neuroscientists annually.

He is currently a member of the Society for Neuroscience and the New York Academy of Sciences. He was the founder of the Learning Brain EXPO and has trained educators and trainers worldwide in this field for 25 years. He is deeply committed to making a positive, lasting difference in the way we learn. Currently, he speaks at conferences and conducts in-school professional development on poverty and engagement. For more information, contact Diane Jensen at diane@jlcbrain.com. In-depth training on achievement and engagement with students from poverty can be found at www.povertysuccess.com.

Related ASCD Resources: Brain-Based Learning and Teaching Students from Poverty

At the time of publication, the following ASCD resources were available (ASCD stock numbers appear in parentheses). For up-to-date information about ASCD resources, go to www.ascd.org.

Multimedia
The Human Brain Professional Inquiry Kit by Bonnie Benesh (#999003)

Networks
Visit the ASCD Web site (www.ascd.org) and click on About ASCD. Go to the section on Networks for information about professional educators who have formed groups around topics such as "Brain-Compatible Learning." Look in the Network Directory for current facilitators' addresses and phone numbers.

Online Courses
Visit the ASCD Web site (www.ascd.org) for the following professional development opportunities:
The Brain: Understanding the Mind (#PD04OC44)
The Brain: Understanding the Physical Brain (#PD99OC05)

Print Products
Arts with the Brain in Mind by Eric Jensen (#101011)
The Best Schools: How Human Development Research Should Inform Educational Practice by Thomas Armstrong (#106044)
The Brain-Compatible Classroom: Using What We Know About Learning to Improve Teaching by Laura Erlauer (#101269)
Brain-Friendly Strategies for the Inclusion Classroom by Judy Willis (#107040)
Brain Matters: Translating Research into Classroom Practice by Patricia Wolfe (#101004)
Discipline with Dignity, 3rd edition: New Challenges, New Solutions by Richard L. Curwin, Allen N. Mendler, and Brian D. Mendler (#108036)
Educational Leadership, May 2007: Educating the Whole Child (#107033)
Educational Leadership, April 2008: Poverty and Learning (#108026)
Educational Leadership, May 2008: Reshaping High Schools (#108027)
Education Update, June 2005: Mental Mileage (#105113)
How to Teach So Students Remember by Marilee Sprenger (#105016)
Preventing Early Learning Failure by Bob Sornson (#101003)
Research-Based Strategies to Ignite Student Learning: Insights from a Neurologist and Classroom Teacher by Judy Willis (#107006)
Teaching the Brain to Read: Strategies for Improving Fluency, Vocabulary, and Comprehension by Judy Willis (#107073)
Teaching to the Brain's Natural Learning Systems by Barbara K. Given (#101075)
Teaching with the Brain in Mind by Eric Jensen (#104013)

Video and DVD
The Brain and Early Childhood (two videotapes with a facilitator's guide) (#400054)
Building Academic Background Knowledge (three programs on one DVD with a facilitator's guide) (#605020)

WHOLE CHILD The Whole Child Initiative helps schools and communities create learning environments that allow students to be healthy, safe, engaged, supported, and challenged. To learn more about other books and resources that relate to the whole child, visit www.wholechildeducation.org.

For more information, visit us on the World Wide Web (http://www.ascd.org); send an e-mail message to member@ascd.org; call the ASCD Service Center (1-800-933-ASCD or 703-578-9600, then press 2); send a fax to 703-575-5400; or write to Information Services, ASCD, 1703 N. Beauregard St., Alexandria, VA 22311-1714 USA.